HAL•LEONARD
ESSENTIAL SONGS

PIANO VOCAL GUITAR

...ngs

ISBN 0-634-09904-3

HAL•LEONARD® CORPORATION
7777 W. BLUEMOUND RD. P.O. BOX 13819 MILWAUKEE, WI 53213

Visit Hal Leonard Online at
www.halleonard.com

CONTENTS

181	Love and Marriage	Married with Children
192	Love Boat Theme	Love Boat
202	MacGyver	MacGyver
197	Theme from "Magnum, P.I."	Magnum, P.I.
204	Major Dad	Major Dad
207	Making Our Dreams Come True	Laverne and Shirley
212	The Masterpiece	Masterpiece Theatre
218	Melrose Place Theme	Melrose Place
220	Miami Vice	Miami Vice
224	The Mighty Mouse Theme (Here I Come to Save the Day)	Mighty Mouse
228	Mission: Impossible Theme	Mission: Impossible
230	Mister Ed	Mister Ed
234	Theme from "The Monkees" (Hey, Hey We're the Monkees)	The Monkees
215	Mork and Mindy	Mork and Mindy
238	The Munsters Theme	The Munsters
240	The Muppet Show Theme	The Muppet Show
246	Murder, She Wrote	Murder, She Wrote
243	Mystery	Mystery
248	NFL on Fox	The NFL on Fox
250	Nadia's Theme	The Young and the Restless
256	The Odd Couple	The Odd Couple
260	Perry Mason Theme	Perry Mason
262	Quantum Leap	Quantum Leap
264	Quincy	Quincy
253	Rawhide	Rawhide
266	The Rockford Files	The Rockford Files
268	Rocky & Bullwinkle	Rocky & Bullwinkle
270	St. Elsewhere	St. Elsewhere
273	Searchin' My Soul	Ally McBeal
278	Secret Agent Man	Secret Agent Man
282	Sesame Street Theme	Sesame Street
288	7th Heaven Main Theme	7th Heaven
290	77 Sunset Strip	77 Sunset Strip
294	Simon and Simon	Simon and Simon
296	Theme from The Simpsons™	The Simpsons™
285	Theme from "Six Million Dollar Man"	Six Million Dollar Man
300	Solid Gold	Solid Gold
304	Song from Buck Rogers	Buck Rogers
307	Theme from Spider Man	Spider Man
310	SpongeBob SquarePants Theme Song	SpongeBob SquarePants
312	Theme from "Star Trek®"	Star Trek®
318	Star Trek - The Next Generation	Star Trek - The Next Generation
315	Tales from the Crypt	Tales from the Crypt
322	This Is It	The Bugs Bunny Show
325	Three's Company Theme	Three's Company
328	The Toy Parade	Leave It to Beaver
334	WKRP in Cincinnati (Main Theme)	WKRP in Cincinnati
336	Welcome Back	Welcome Back Kotter
331	Where Everybody Knows Your Name	Cheers
340	Wings	Wings
342	Without Us	Family Ties
368	Woke Up This Morning	The Sopranos
348	Won't You Be My Neighbor? (It's a Beautiful Day in This Neighborhood)	Mr. Rogers' Neighborhood
350	Woody Woodpecker	Woody Woodpecker
354	Xena: Warrior Princess	Xena: Warrior Princess
358	The X-Files	The X-Files
364	Yakety Sax	The Benny Hill Show

THEME FROM "THE A TEAM"
from the Television Series

By MIKE POST
and PETE CARPENTER

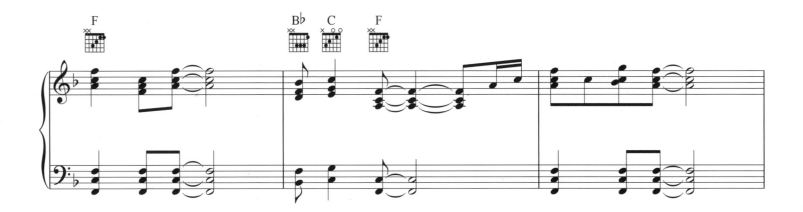

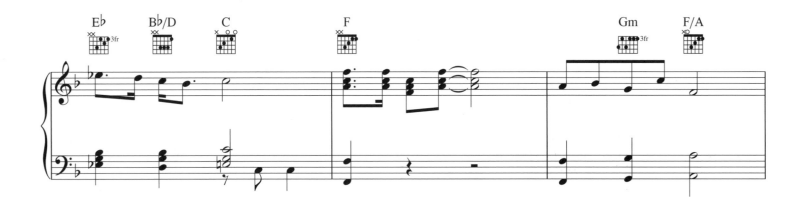

ALFRED HITCHCOCK PRESENTS
Theme from the Television Series

By D. KAHN
and M. LENARD

Mysteriously

THE ADDAMS FAMILY THEME

Theme from the TV Show and Movie

Music and Lyrics by
VIC MIZZY

AMERICAN IDOL THEME

Words and Music by JULIAN GINGELL,
BARRY STONE and CATHY DENNIS

Moderately fast

8vb throughout

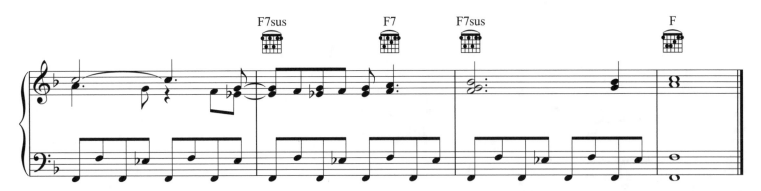

* *Recorded a half step higher.*

THE AVENGERS THEME

from the Warner Bros. Pictures' Presentation THE AVENGERS

Words and Music by
LAURIE JOHNSON

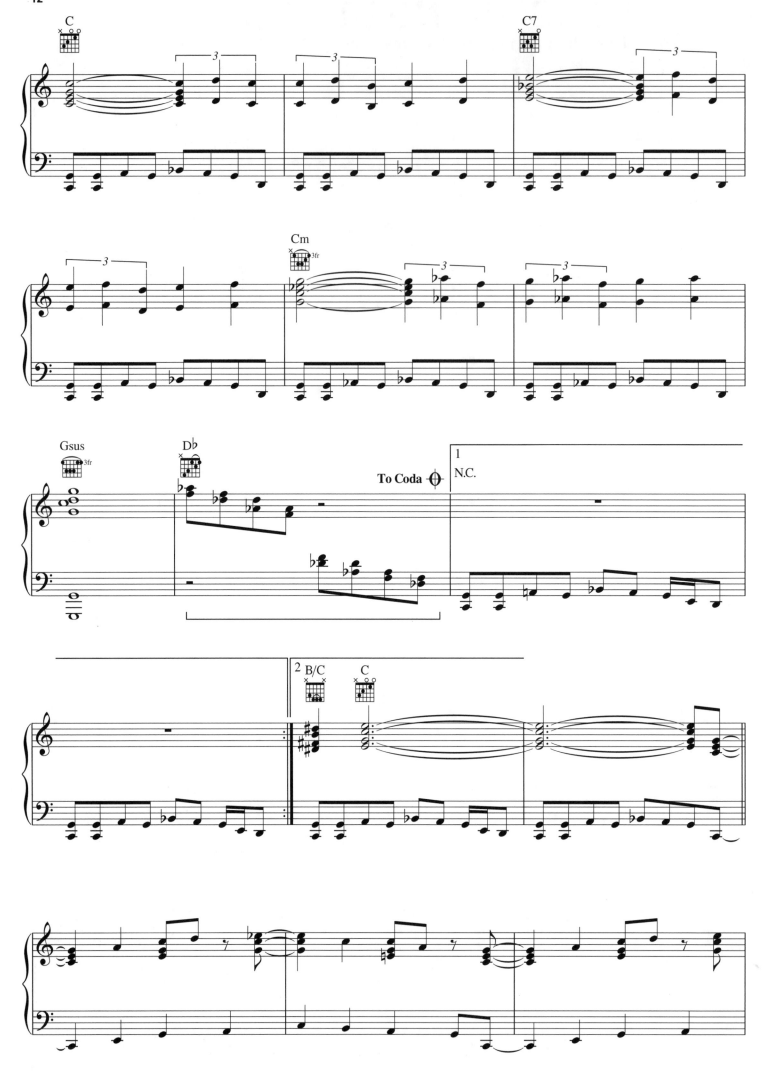

ANGELA
Theme from the Paramount Television Series TAXI

By BOB JAMES

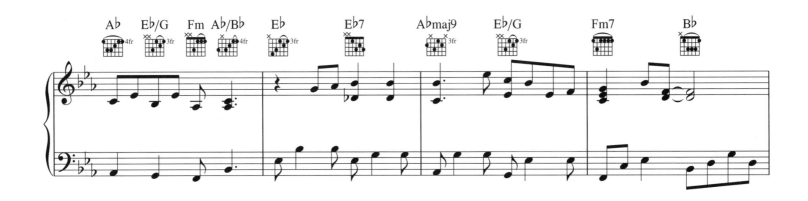

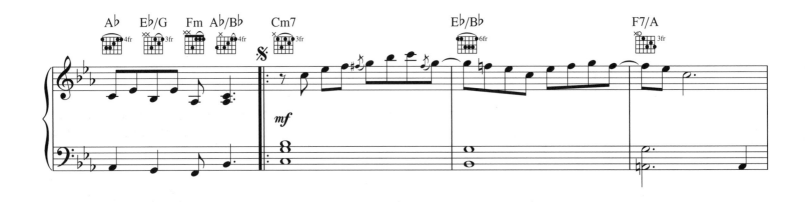

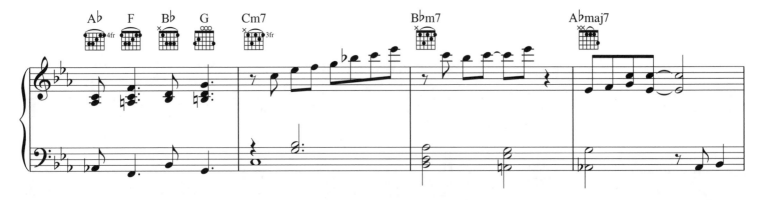

17

BANDSTAND BOOGIE
from the Television Series AMERICAN BANDSTAND

Special Lyric by BARRY MANILOW and BRUCE SUSSMAN
Music by CHARLES ALBERTINE

We're go-in' hop-pin'! (Hop!) We're go-in'
swing-in'! (Swing!) We're gon-na

hop-pin' to-day, where things are pop-pin' (Pop!) the Phil-a-del-phi-a way. We're gon-na
swing in the crowd, and we'll be cling-in' (Cling!) and float-in' high on a cloud. The phones are

THEME FROM BARNABY JONES

from the Television Series BARNABY JONES

By JERRY GOLDSMITH

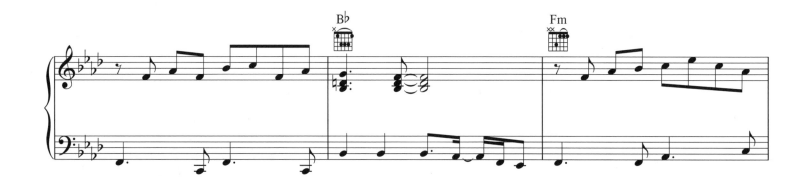

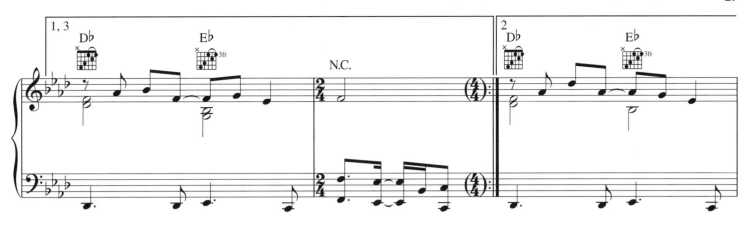

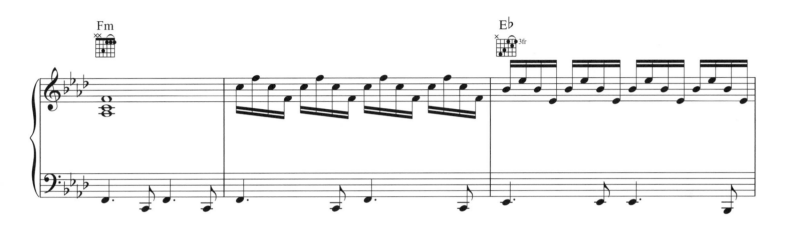

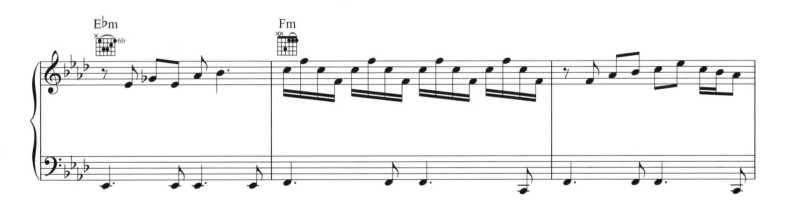

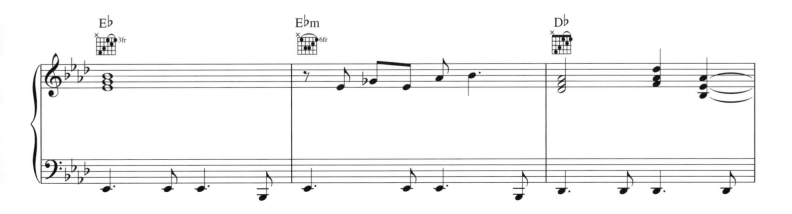

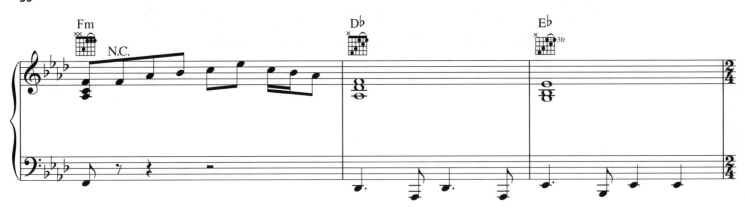

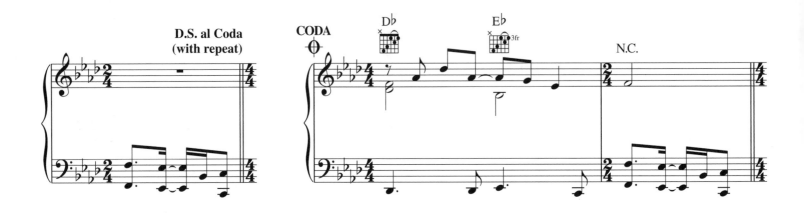

BATTLESTAR GALACTICA
Theme from the Universal Television Series BATTLESTAR GALACTICA

By STU PHILLIPS
and GLEN LARSON

Majestically

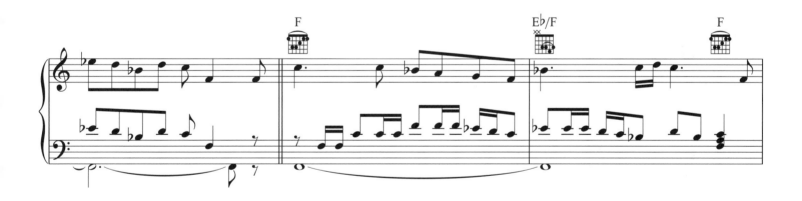

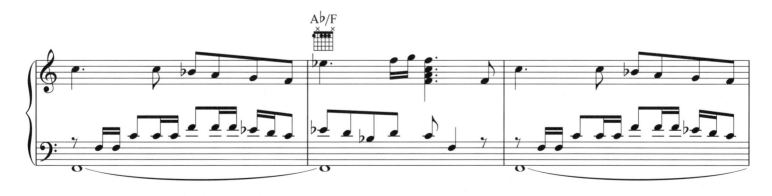

A little slower

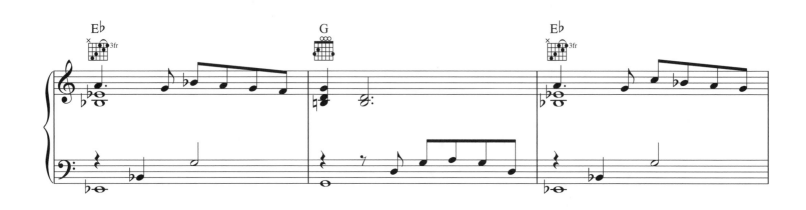

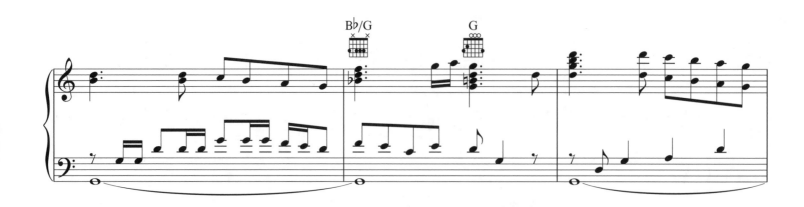

BEAVIS AND BUTTHEAD THEME (TV)

from the Televeision Series BEAVIS AND BUTTHEAD

Written by MIKE JUDGE

BEVERLY HILLS 90210
(Main Theme)
from the Television Series BEVERLY HILLS 90210

By JOHN E. DAVIS

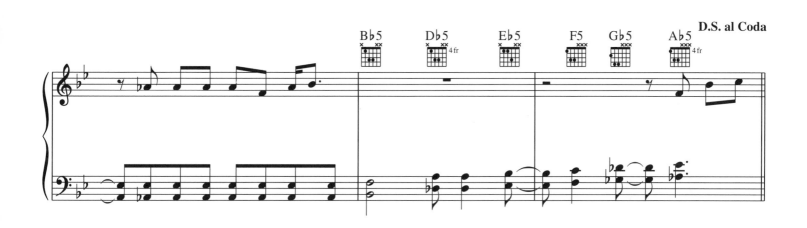

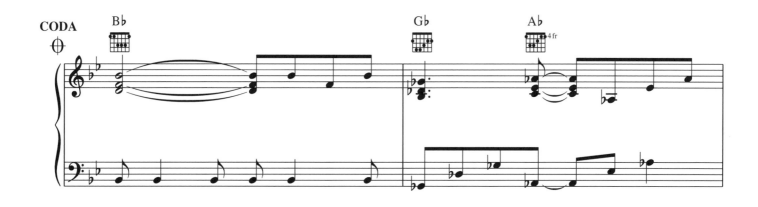

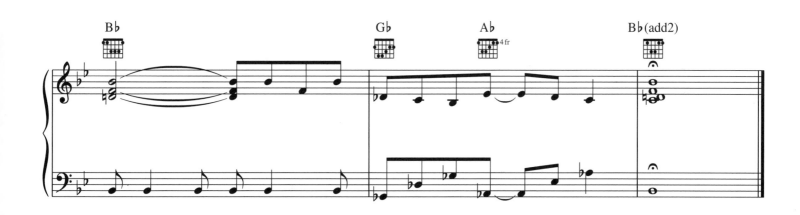

THEME FROM "BEWITCHED"
from the Television Series

Words and Music by JACK KELLER
and HOWARD GREENFIELD

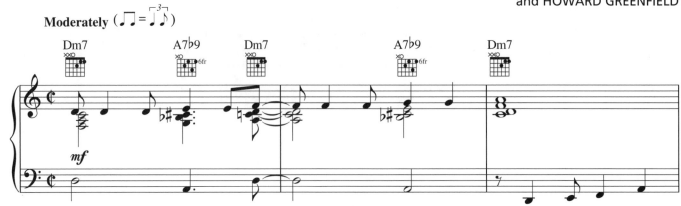

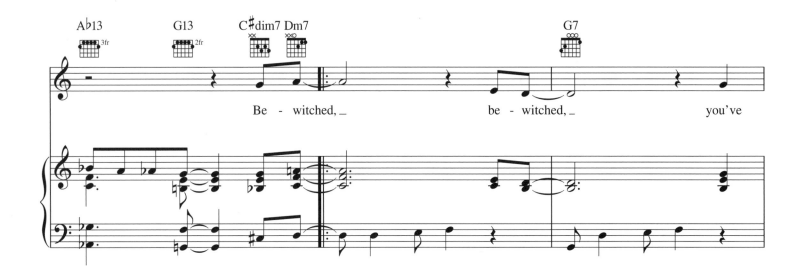

Be - witched, _ be - witched, _ you've

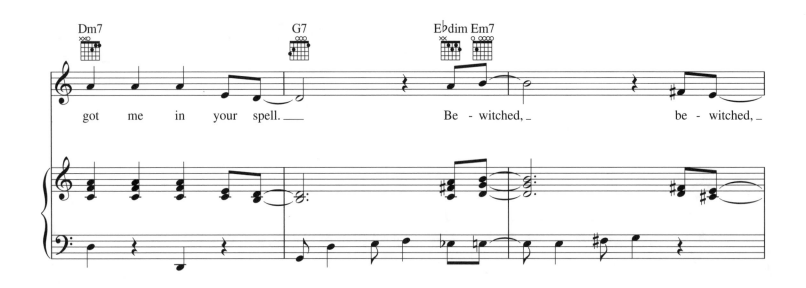

got me in your spell. ___ Be - witched, _ be - witched, _

could be had ___ but now I'm caught and I'm ___ kind-a glad ___ to be ___

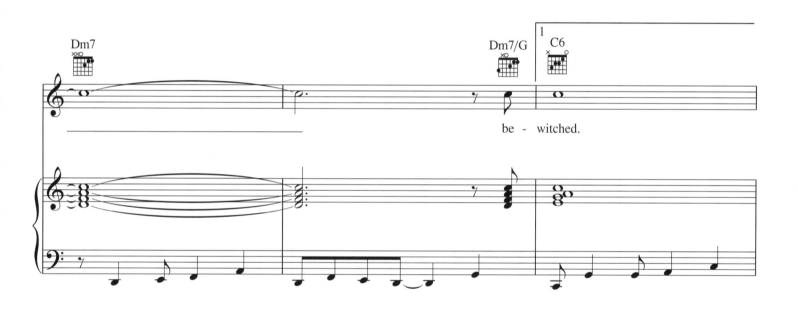

be - witched.

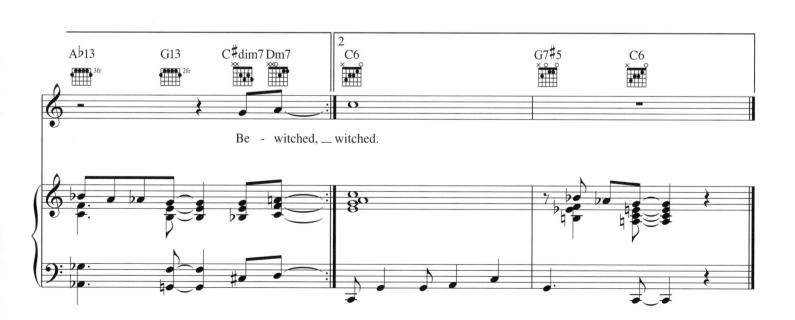

Be - witched, ___ witched.

BOB THE BUILDER
"Intro Theme Song"
from the Television Series BOB THE BUILDER

Words and Music by
PAUL JOYCE

44

46

BONANZA
Theme from the TV Series

Words and Music by JAY LIVINGSTON
and RAY EVANS

BOSS OF ME
(Theme from Malcolm In The Middle)
from MALCOLM IN THE MIDDLE

By JOHN FLANSBURGH
and JOHN LINNELL

You're not the boss of me ___ now, and you're not so big.

THE BRADY BUNCH
Theme from the Paramount Television Series THE BRADY BUNCH

Words and Music by SHERWOOD SCHWARTZ
and FRANK DEVOL

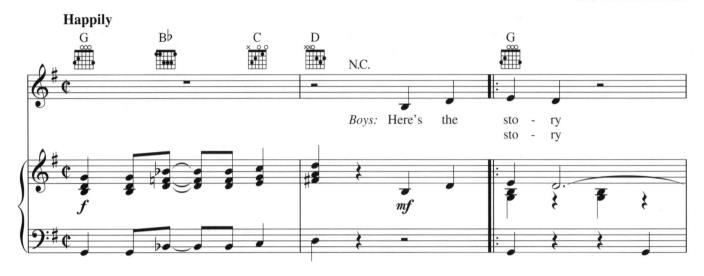

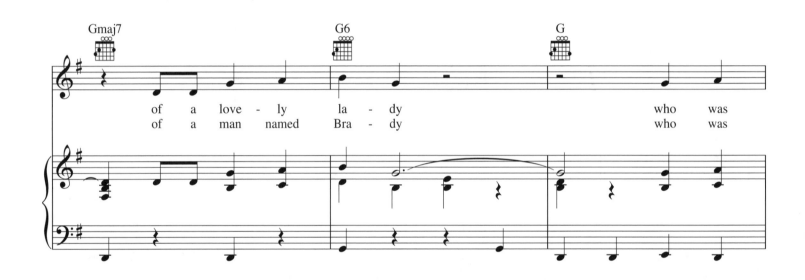

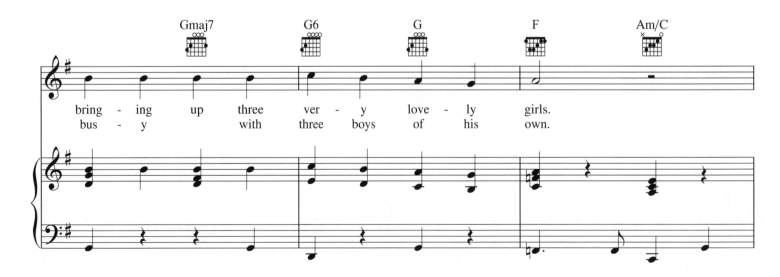

THEME FROM BUFFY THE VAMPIRE SLAYER

from the Twentieth Century Fox Television Series BUFFY THE VAMPIRE SLAYER

By CHARLES DENNIS,
PARRY GRIPP and STEPHEN SHERLOCK

Fast Punk Rock

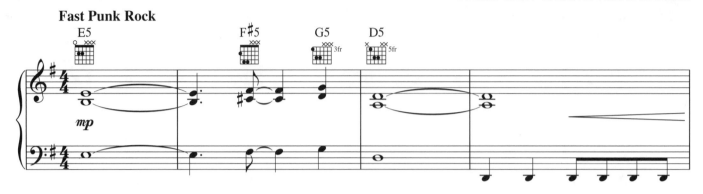

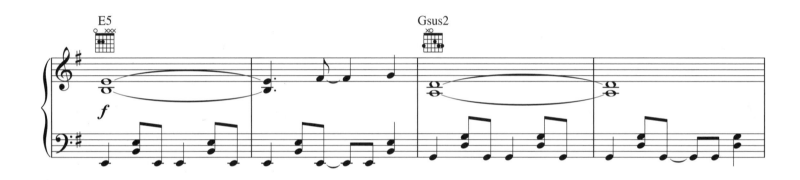

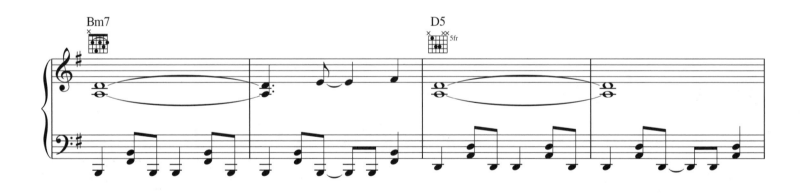

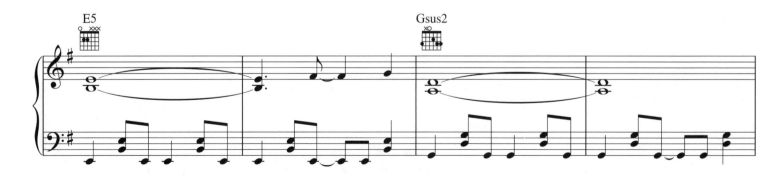

CHICAGO HOPE

from the Twentieth Century Fox Television Series CHICAGO HOPE

By MARK ISHAM

CLEVELAND ROCKS
Theme from THE DREW CAREY SHOW

Words and Music by
IAN HUNTER

THEME FROM COLUMBO

from the Television Series COLUMBO

By BILLY GOLDENBERG

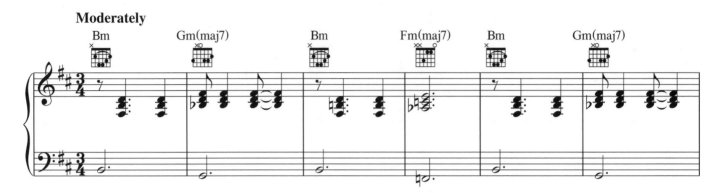

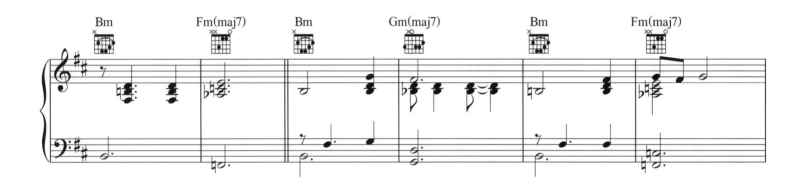

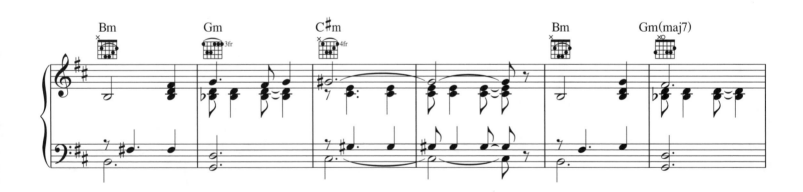

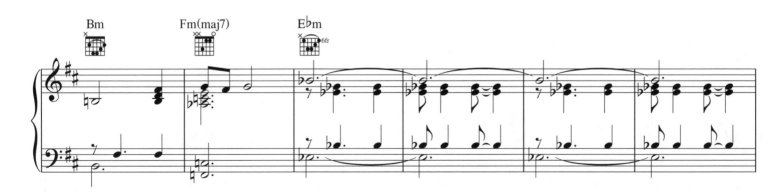

COME ON GET HAPPY

Theme from THE PARTRIDGE FAMILY

Words and Music by WES FARRELL
and DANNY JANSSEN

DENNIS THE MENACE

from the Television Series DENNIS THE MENACE

Words and Music by WILLIAM LOOSE
and JOHN SEELY

Den - nis, that's my name, but some call me the men - ace.

Instrumental on D.S.

Why? I'll nev - er know. 'Cause I'm so harm - less; harm - less as a pup - py and

care - free as a gup - py a - swim-min' round the pond. Skip - py do and skip - py dum.

Sung both times

DESPERATE HOUSEWIVES MAIN TITLE

By DANNY ELFMAN

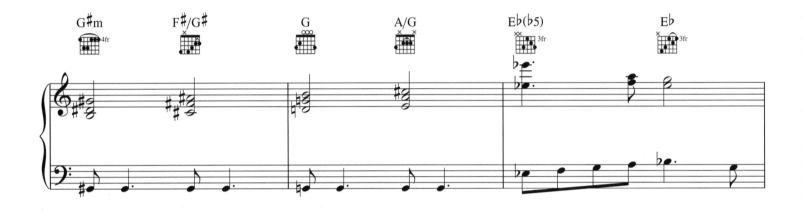

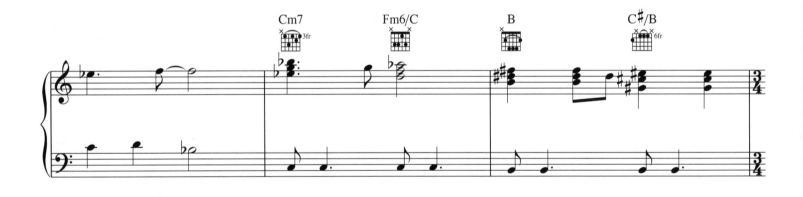

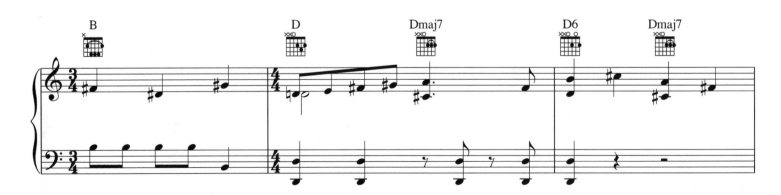

DICK VAN DYKE SHOW THEME

from the Television Series the DICK VAN DYKE SHOW

By EARLE HAGEN

Moderately, with a beat

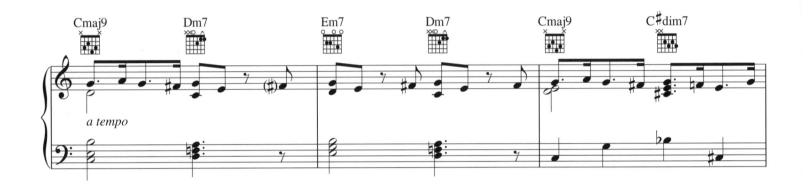

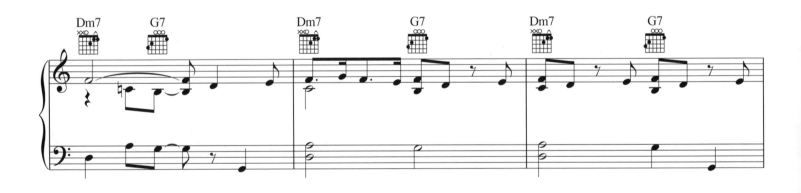

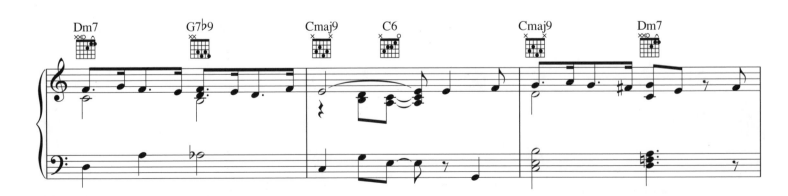

DOOGIE HOWSER, M.D. THEME

from the Steven Bochco Productions Televison Series DOOGIE HOWSER, M.D.

By MIKE POST

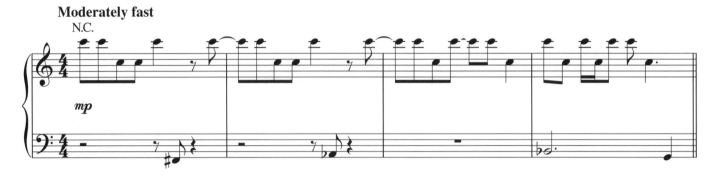

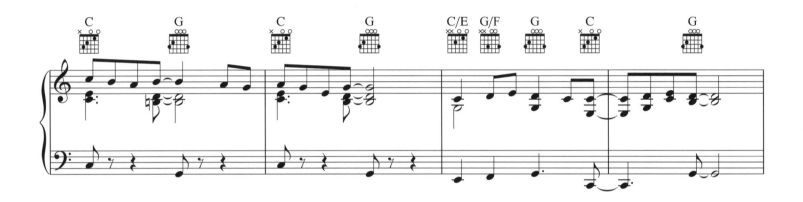

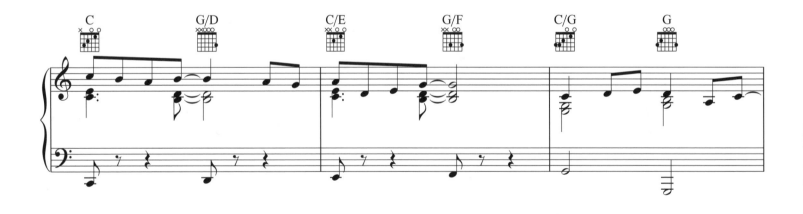

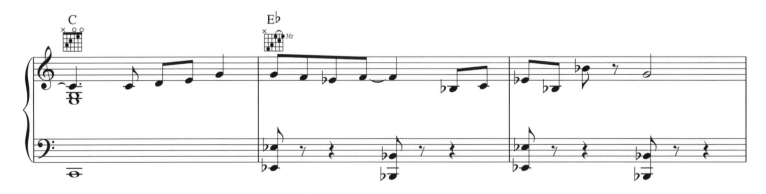

DRAGNET

Words and Music by WALTER SCHUMANN
and MIKLOS ROSZA

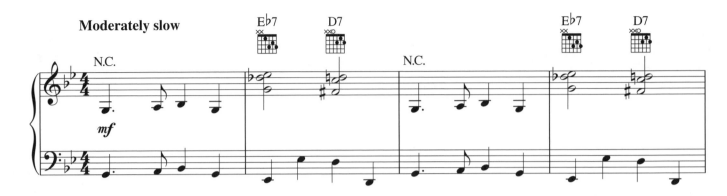

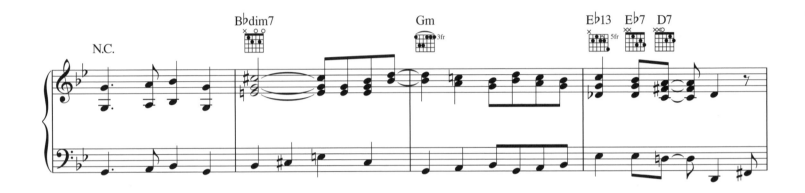

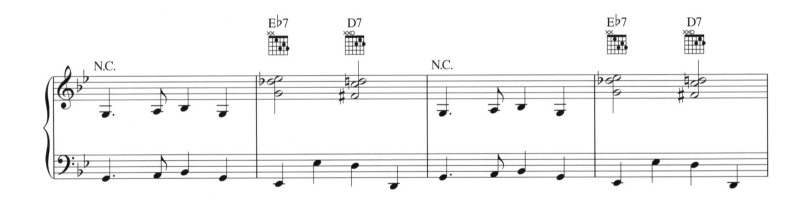

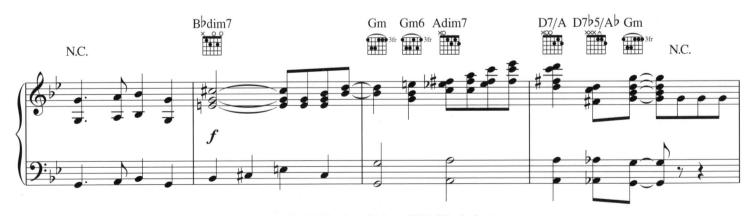

DYNASTY THEME

from DYNASTY

By BILL CONTI

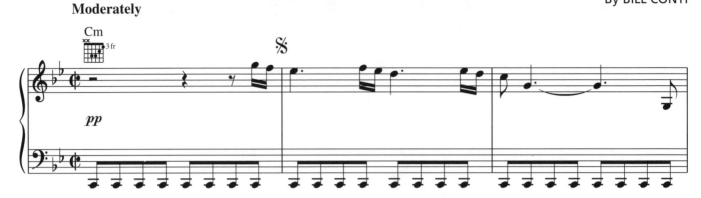

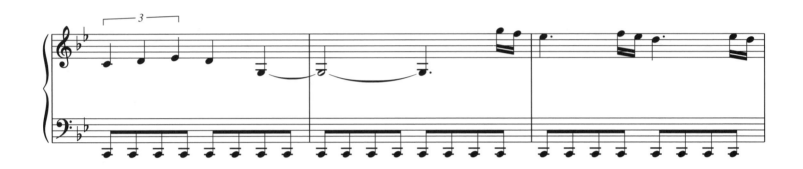

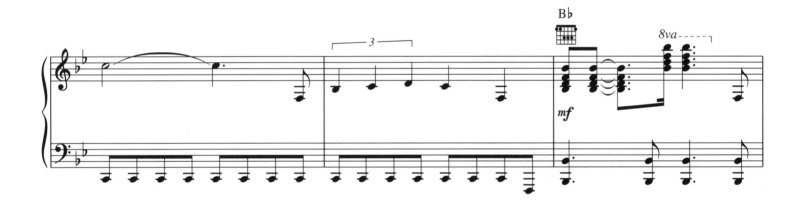

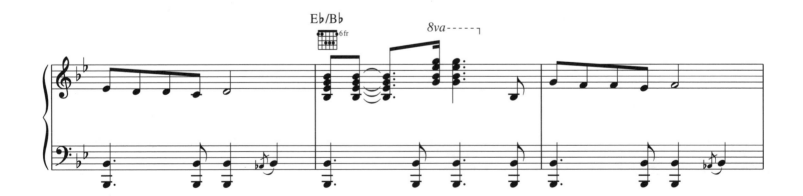

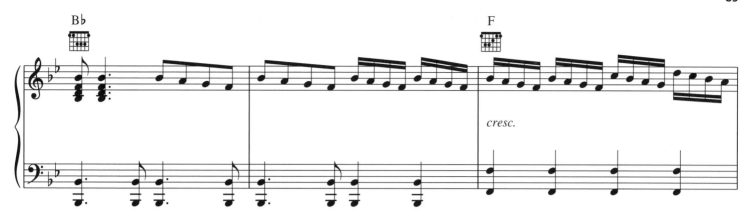

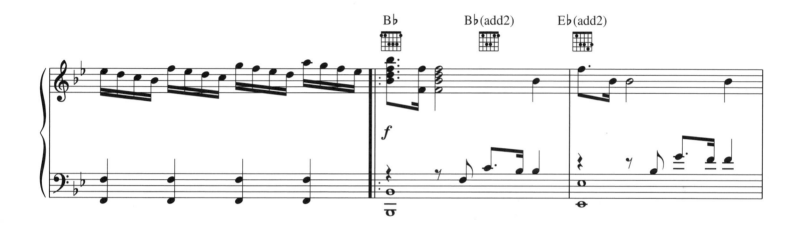

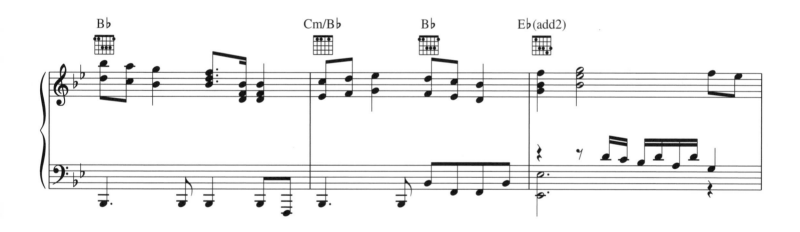

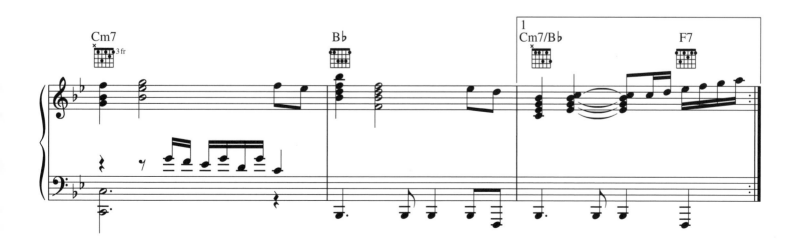

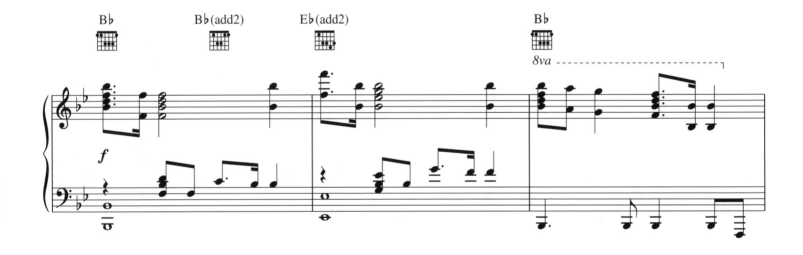

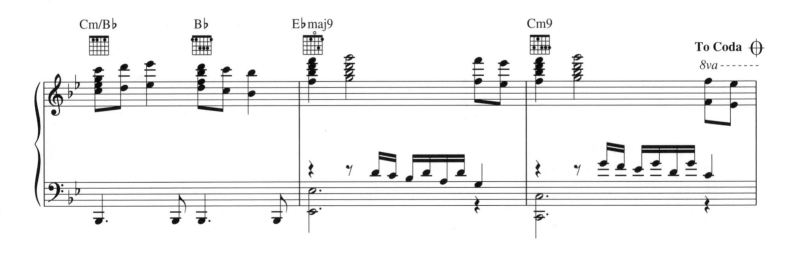

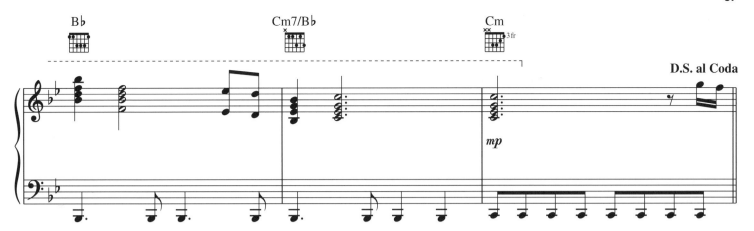

ENTERTAINMENT TONIGHT
Theme from the Paramount Television Show

Music by MICHAEL MARK

Moderately fast

GOOD OLD DAYS
(Little Rascals Theme)
Theme from LITTLE RASCALS

By ROY SHIELD

THEME FROM FAMILY GUY

from the Twentieth Century Fox Television Series FAMILY GUY

Words by SETH MacFARLANE and DAVID ZUCKERMAN
Music by WALTER MURPHY

Moderately fast

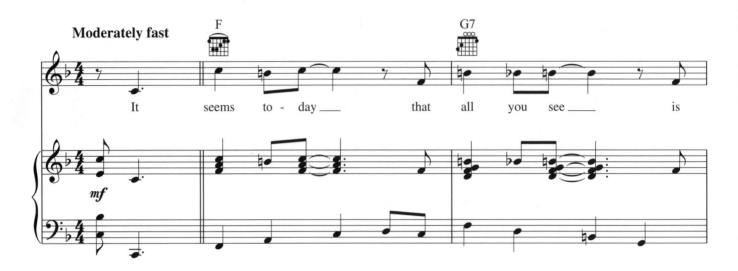

It seems to-day ___ that all you see ___ is

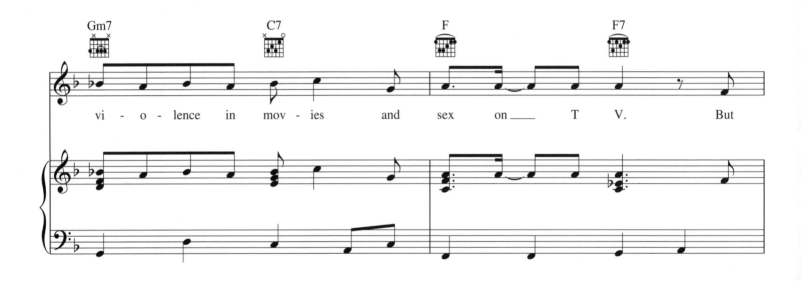

vi - o - lence in mov - ies and sex on ___ T. V. But

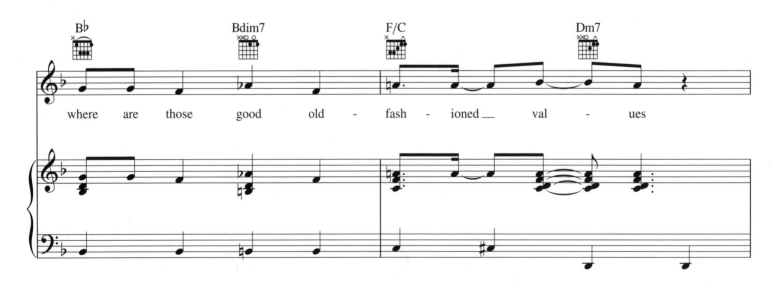

where are those good old - fash - ioned ___ val - ues

THEME FROM "FRASIER"
from the Paramount Television Series FRASIER

Words by DARRYL PHINNESSEE
Music by BRUCE MILLER

hear the blues a-call-in' tossed sal-ads and scram-bled eggs, __

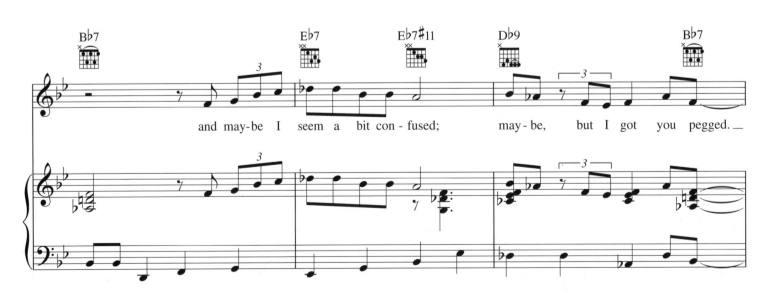

and may-be I seem a bit con-fused; may-be, but I got you pegged. __

FUTURAMA THEME

from the Television Series FUTURAMA

By CHRISTOPHER TYNG

THEME FROM
"THE GREATEST AMERICAN HERO"

from the Television Series

Words by STEPHEN GEYER
Music by MIKE POST

GREEN ACRES THEME

from the Television Series GREEN ACRES

Music and Lyrics by
VIC MIZZY

HAPPY DAYS

Theme from the Paramount Television Series HAPPY DAYS

Words by NORMAN GIMBEL
Music by CHARLES FOX

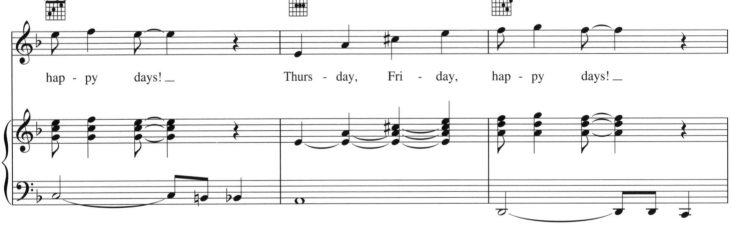

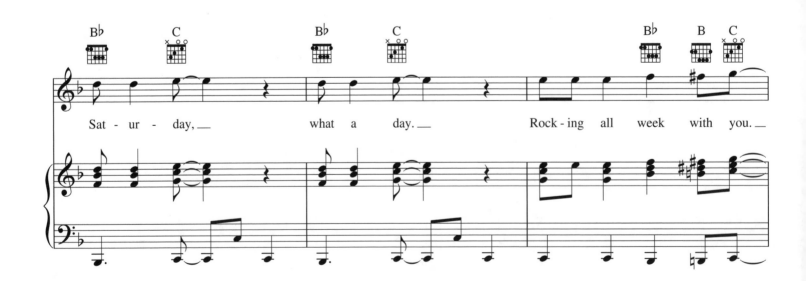

HAPPY TRAILS

from the Television Series THE ROY ROGERS SHOW

Words and Music by
DALE EVANS

HARLEM NOCTURNE

featured in the Television Series MIKE HAMMER

Music by EARLE HAGEN
Words by DICK ROGERS

HERCULES:
THE LEGENDARY JOURNEYS

from the Television Series HERCULES: THE LEGENDARY JOURNEYS

By JOSEPH LoDUCA

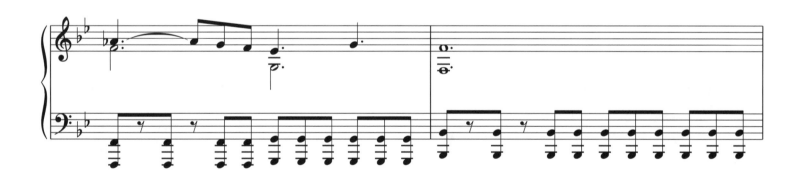

HERE WITH ME
Theme from ROSWELL

Lyrics by DIDO ARMSTRONG
Music by DIDO ARMSTRONG,
PAUL STATHAM and PASCAL GABRIEL

HILL STREET BLUES THEME
from the Television Series

By MIKE POST

Slowly, freely

Moderately

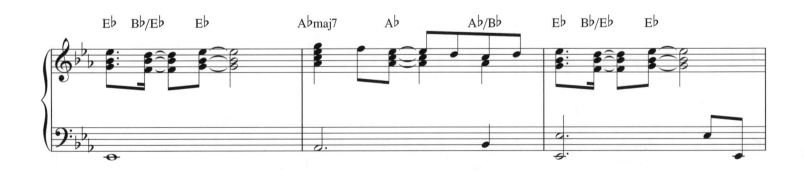

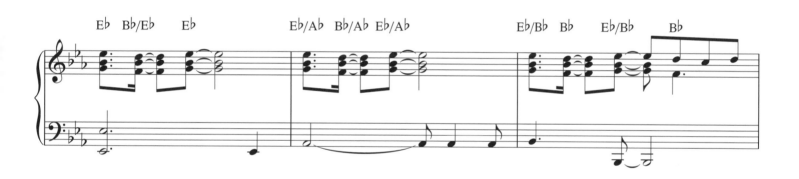

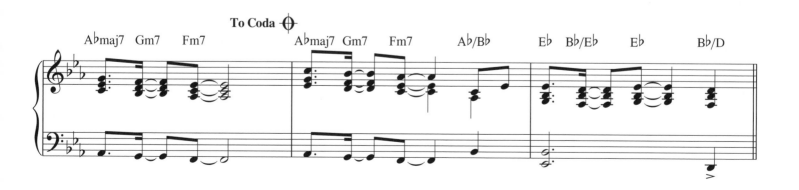

130

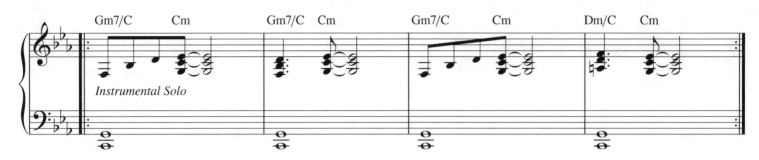

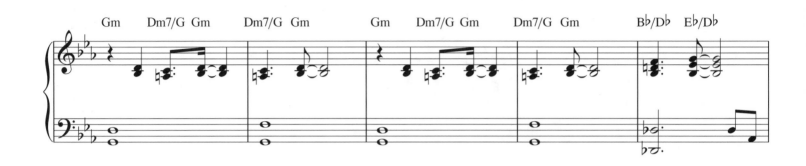

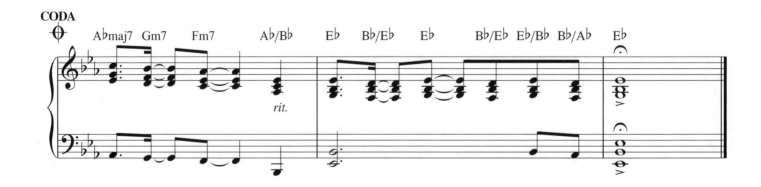

I LOVE LUCY
from the Television Series

Lyric by HAROLD ADAMSON
Music by ELIOT DANIEL

Lyrics:
I love Lu - cy and she loves me, we're as hap - py as two can be. Some - times we quar - rel but then, _____

HOGAN'S HEROES MARCH

from the Television Series HOGAN'S HEROES

By JERRY FIELDING

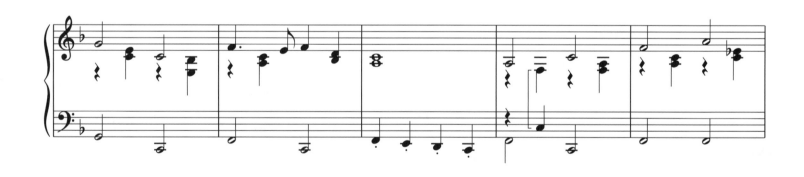

135

I DON'T WANT TO WAIT
featured in DAWSON'S CREEK

Words and Music by
PAULA COLE

So o-pen up your morn-ing light and say a lit-tle prayer for I. You know that

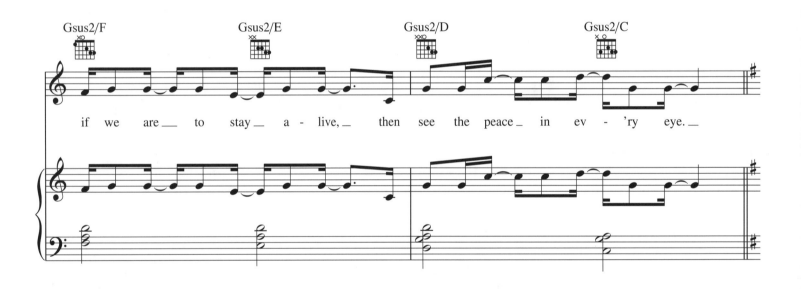

if we are to stay a-live, then see the peace in ev-'ry eye.

Du du du du du, du du du du du,

I'M ALWAYS HERE
Theme from BAYWATCH

Words and Music by JOHN D'ANDREA,
JOE HENRY, JIM JAMISON
and CORY LERIOS

here.

D.S. al Coda

'Cause

I'M POPEYE THE SAILOR MAN
Theme from the Paramount Cartoon POPEYE THE SAILOR

Words and Music by
SAMMY LERNER

I'M SO GLAD WE HAD THIS TIME TOGETHER

Carol Burnett's Theme from THE CAROL BURNETT SHOW

By JOE HAMILTON

JEANNIE
Theme from I DREAM OF JEANNIE

By HUGH MONTENEGRO
and BUDDY KAYE

THE INCREDIBLE HULK
Theme from the Universal Television Series THE INCREDIBLE HULK

By JOE HARNELL

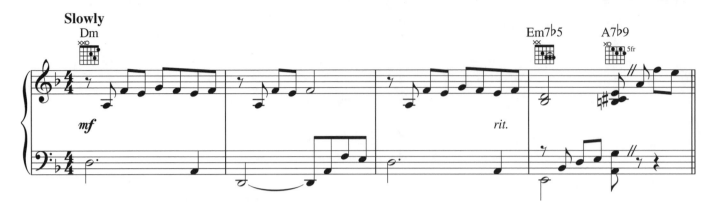

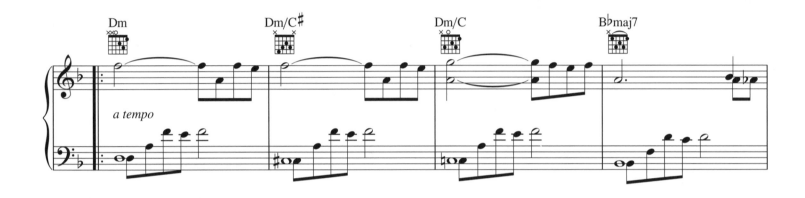

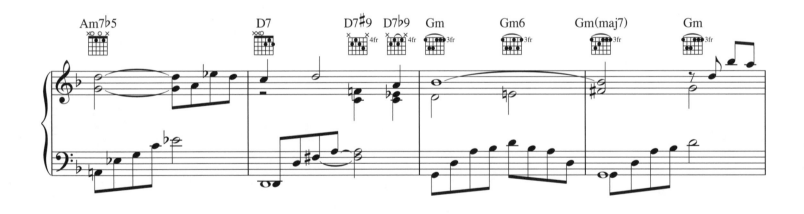

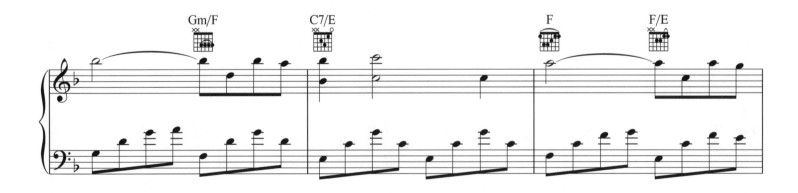

IT'S HOWDY DOODY TIME
Theme from THE HOWDY DOODY SHOW

Words and Music by
EDWARD GEORGE KEAN

Up-tempo March

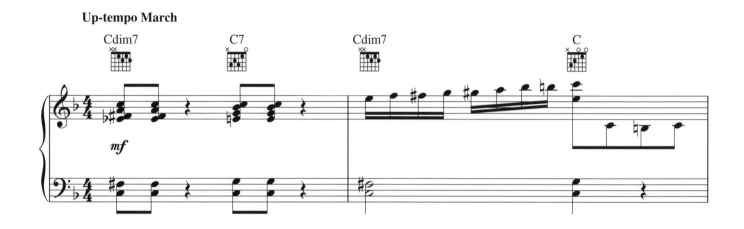

JEOPARDY THEME

from the Television Game Show Jeopardy!

Music by MERV GRIFFIN

Moderately bright

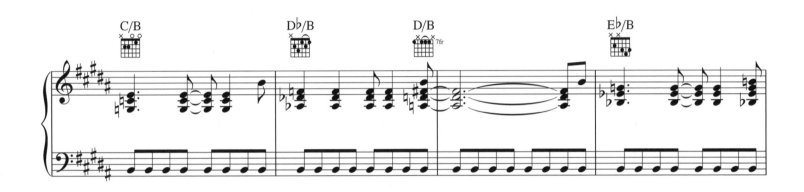

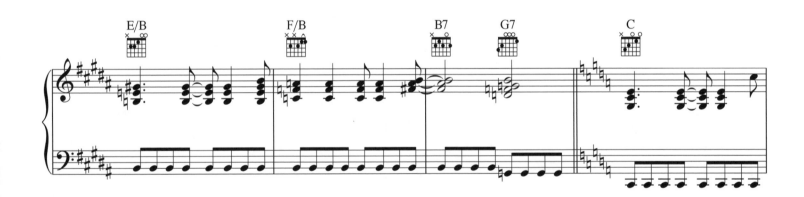

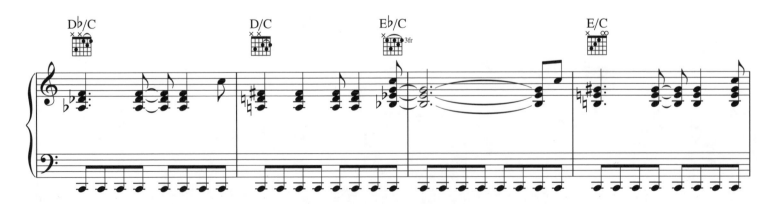

KNIGHT RIDER THEME

from the Television Series KNIGHT RIDER

By STU PHILLIPS
and GLEN LARSON

Moderately fast

JOHNNY'S THEME
from THE TONIGHT SHOW

Words and Music by PAUL ANKA
and JOHNNY CARSON

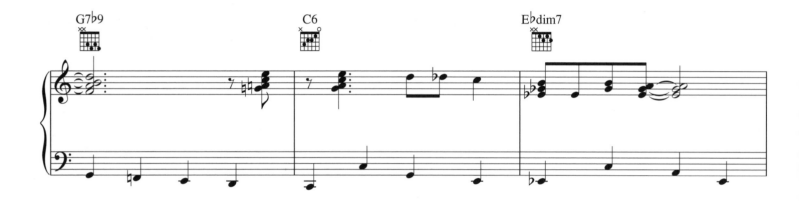

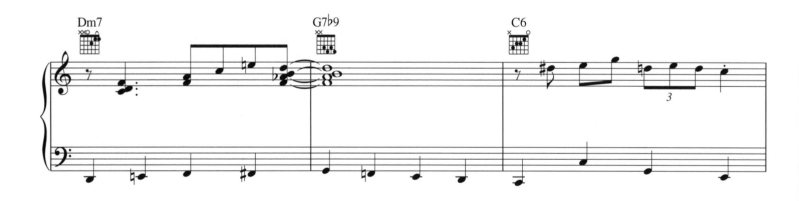

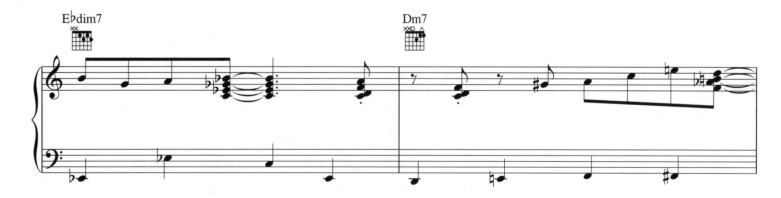

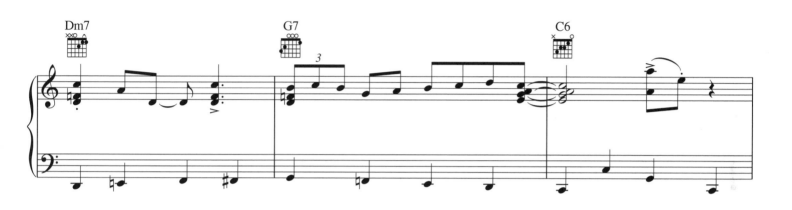

THEME FROM KING OF THE HILL

from the Twentieth Century Fox Television Series KING OF THE HILL

By ROGER CLYNE, BRIAN BLUSH,
ARTHUR EDWARDS and PAUL NAFFAH

Moderately fast Rock

LAW AND ORDER

from the Television Series LAW AND ORDER

By MIKE POST

LIBERTY BELL MARCH
from MONTY PYTHON'S FLYING CIRCUS

By JOHN PHILIP SOUSA

8va basso

LOVE AND MARRIAGE

from the Television Series MARRIED WITH CHILDREN

Words by SAMMY CAHN
Music by JAMES VAN HEUSEN

LINUS AND LUCY
from A BOY NAMED CHARLIE BROWN

By VINCE GUARALDI

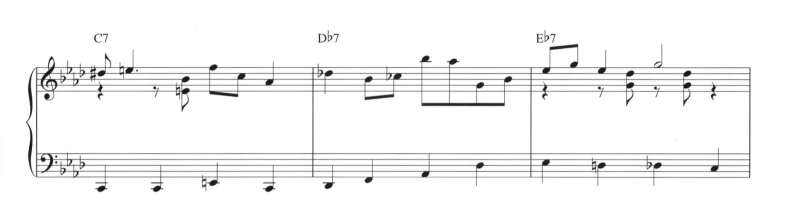

Original Tempo (♩♩ = ♩♩)

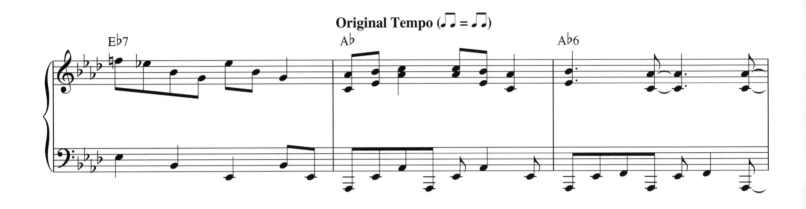

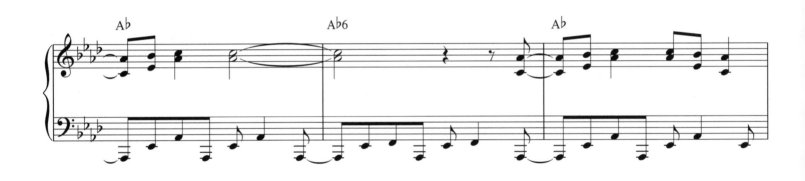

THE LITTLE HOUSE
(On the Prairie)
Theme from the TV Series

Music by DAVID ROSE

LOVE BOAT THEME

from the Television Series

Words and Music by CHARLES FOX
and PAUL WILLIAMS

THEME FROM "MAGNUM, P.I."

from the Universal Television Series MAGNUM, P.I.

By MIKE POST
and PETE CARPENTER

201

MacGYVER
Theme from the Paramount T.V. Series MacGYVER

Words and Music by
RANDY EDELMAN

Bright Rock

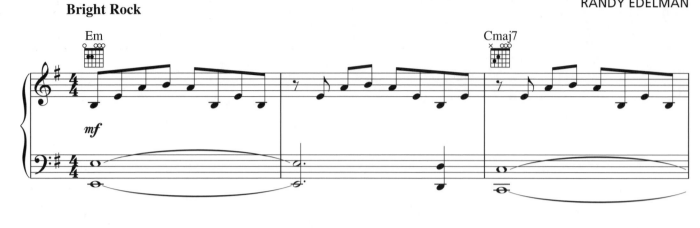

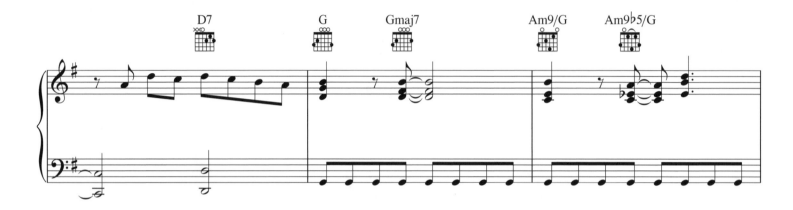

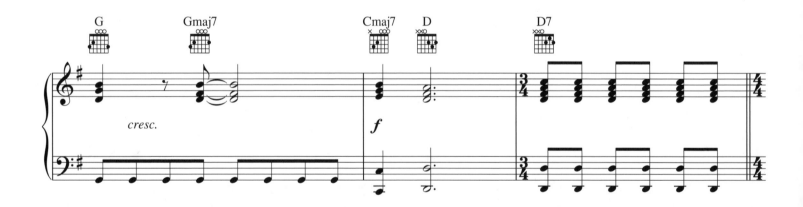

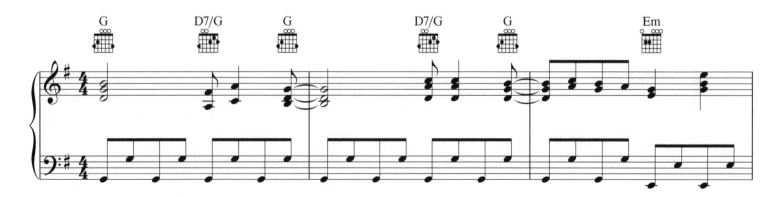

MAJOR DAD
Theme from the Television Series

By ROGER STEINMAN

Spirited march

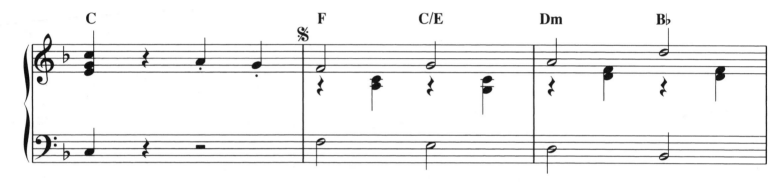

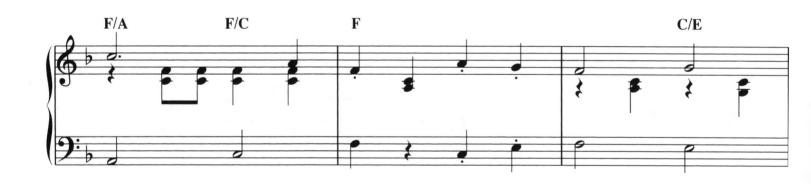

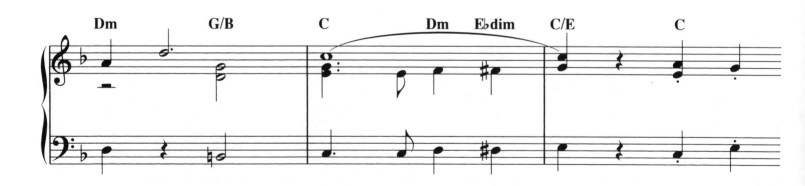

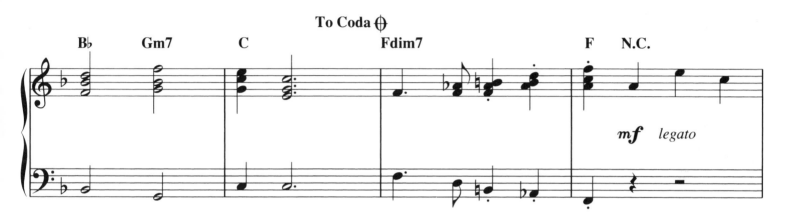

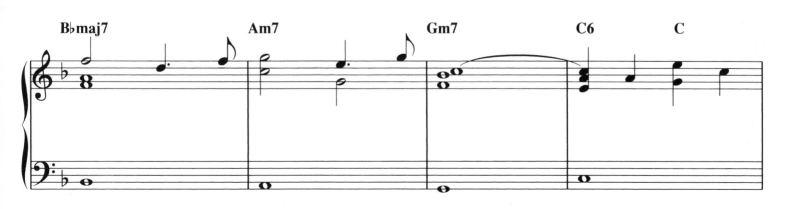

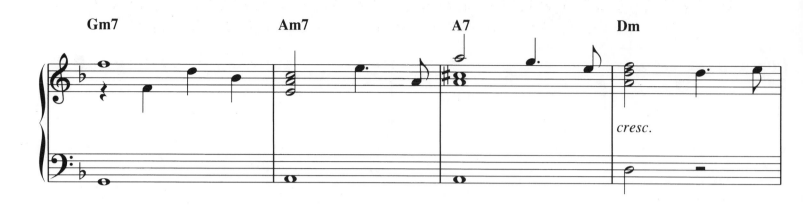

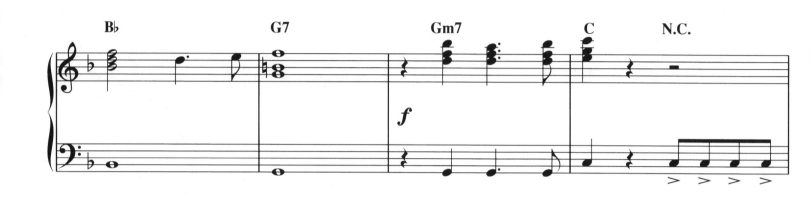

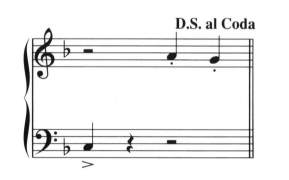

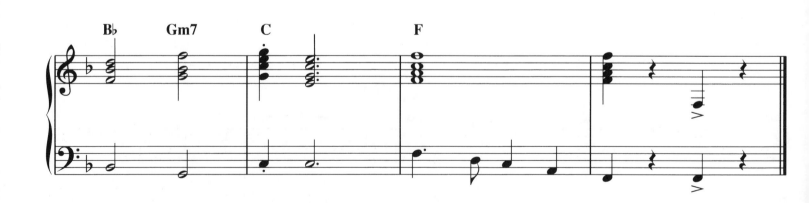

MAKING OUR DREAMS COME TRUE

Theme from the Paramount Television Series LAVERNE AND SHIRLEY

Words by NORMAN GIMBEL
Music by CHARLES FOX

Bright 4

One two three four five six sev-en eight shle-miel ___ shle-maz-el ___

has-en-fe-fer in-cor-po-rat-ed. We're gon-na do ___ it! Give us an-y chance, ___

___ we'll take ___ it. Read us an-y rule, ___ we'll break ___ it.

THE MASTERPIECE
the TV Theme from MASTERPIECE THEATRE

By J.J. MOURET
and PAUL PARNES

Majestically

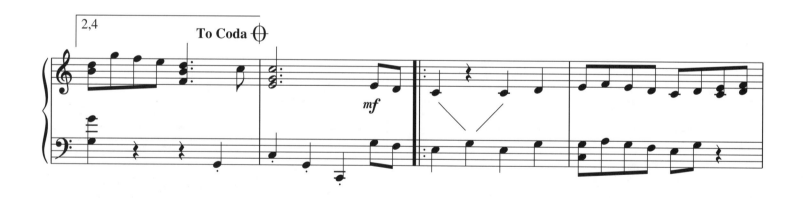

MORK AND MINDY

Theme from the Paramount Television Series MORK AND MINDY

By PERRY BOTKIN, JR.

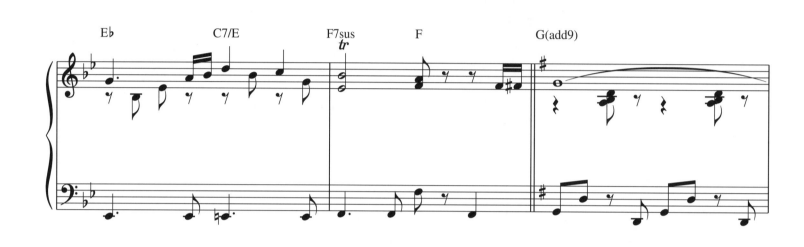

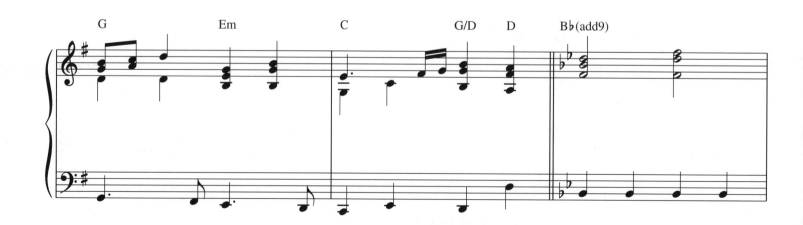

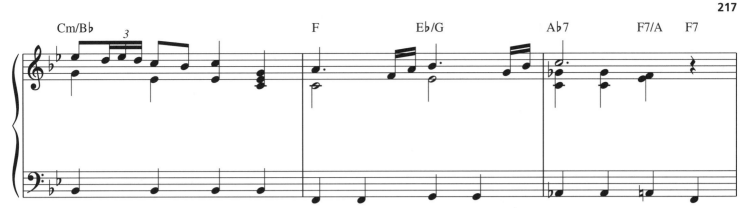

MELROSE PLACE THEME

from the Television Series MELROSE PLACE

By TIM TRUMAN

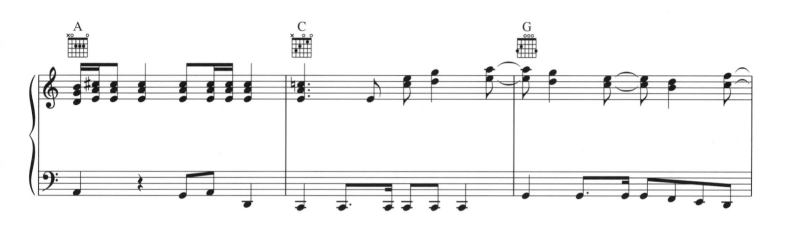

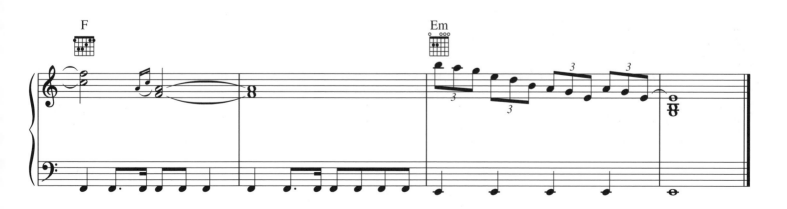

MIAMI VICE
Theme from the Universal Television Series

By JAN HAMMER

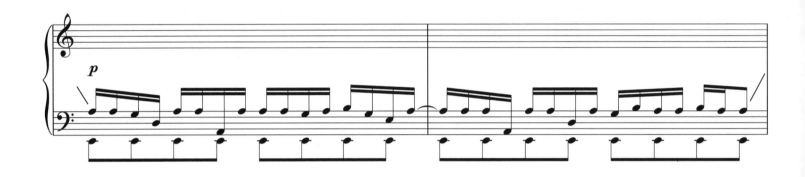

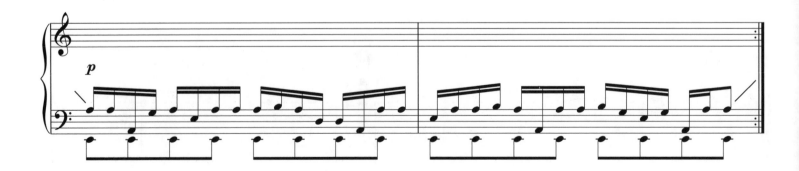

THE MIGHTY MOUSE THEME
(Here I Come to Save the Day)
from the Television Series MIGHTY MOUSE

Words by MARSHALL BARER
Music by PHILLIP SCHIEB

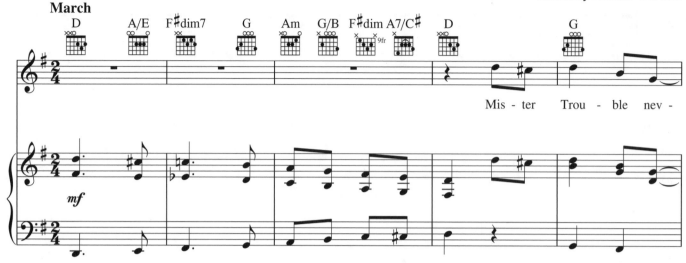

way.

Might-y Mouse is on the way.

MISSION: IMPOSSIBLE THEME

from the Paramount Television Series MISSION: IMPOSSIBLE

By LALO SCHIFRIN

Moderately, with drive

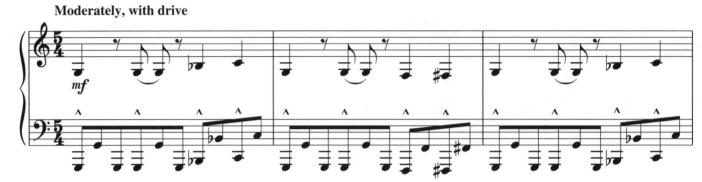

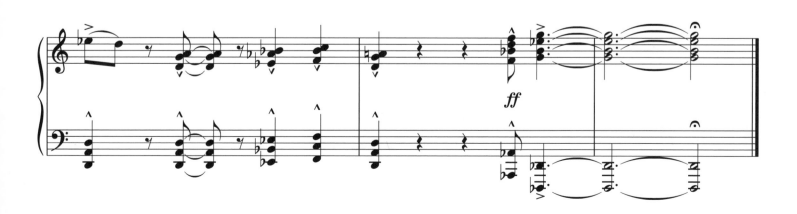

MISTER ED
from the Television Series

Words and Music by JAY LIVINGSTON
and RAY EVANS

THEME FROM "THE MONKEES"
(Hey, Hey We're the Monkees)
from the Television Series THE MONKEES

Words and Music by TOMMY BOYCE
and BOBBY HART

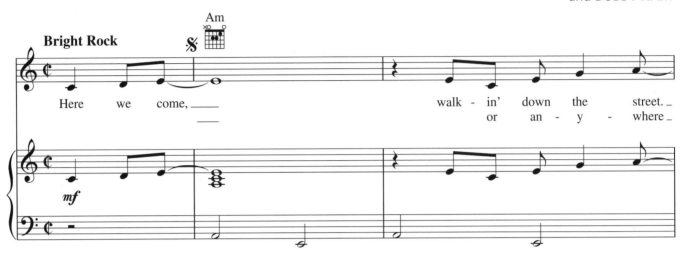

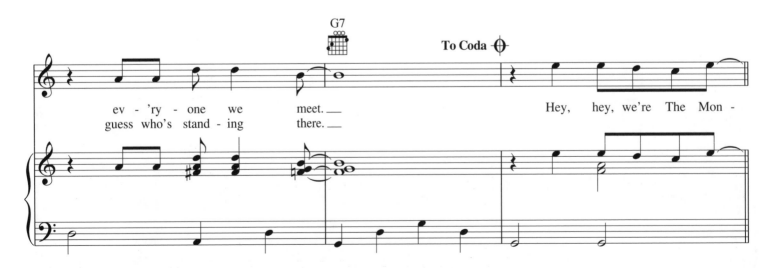

THE MUNSTERS THEME

from the Television Series

By JACK MARSHALL

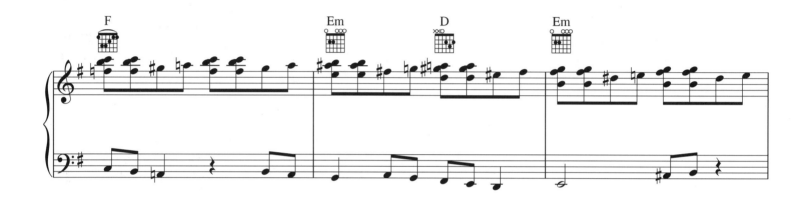

THE MUPPET SHOW THEME

from the Television Series

Words and Music by JIM HENSON
and SAM POTTLE

MYSTERY
Theme from the PBS Television Series

Music by NORMAND ROGER

MURDER, SHE WROTE

Theme from the Universal Television Series MURDER, SHE WROTE

Music by JOHN ADDISON

NFL ON FOX THEME
from the Fox Sports Broadcasts of THE NFL ON FOX

By PHIL GARROD,
REED HAYS and SCOTT SCHREER

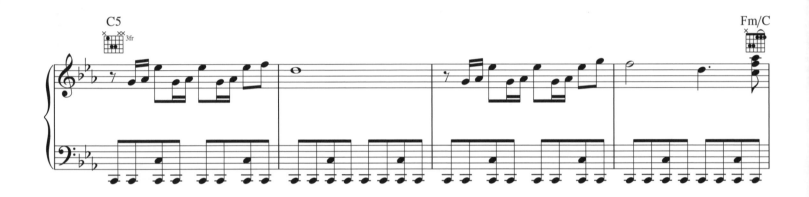

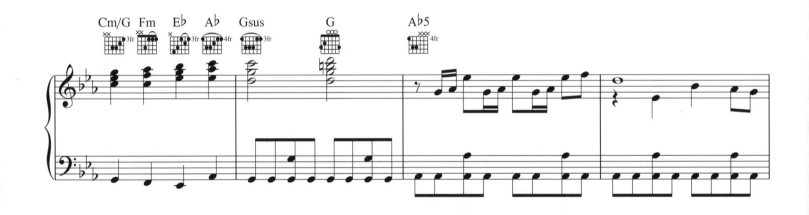

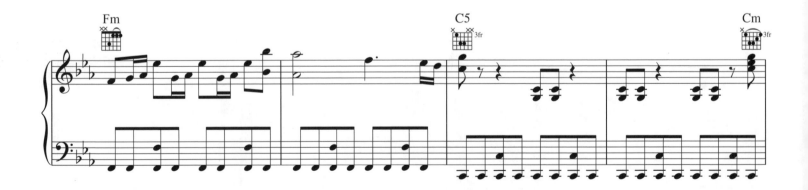

NADIA'S THEME
from THE YOUNG AND THE RESTLESS

By BARRY DeVORZON
and PERRY BOTKIN, JR.

RAWHIDE

from the Television Series RAWHIDE

Words and Music by DIMITRI TIOMKIN
and NED WASHINGTON

254

THE ODD COUPLE

Theme from the Paramount Picture THE ODD COUPLE

Words by SAMMY CAHN
Music by NEAL HEFTI

Moderately, with a steady beat

No mat-ter where they go, _____ they are known as the cou - ple. _____

They're nev - er seen a - lone, _____ so they're known as the cou - ple. _____

PERRY MASON THEME
from the Television Series

By FRED STEINER

261

QUANTUM LEAP
from the Television Series QUANTUM LEAP

By MIKE POST

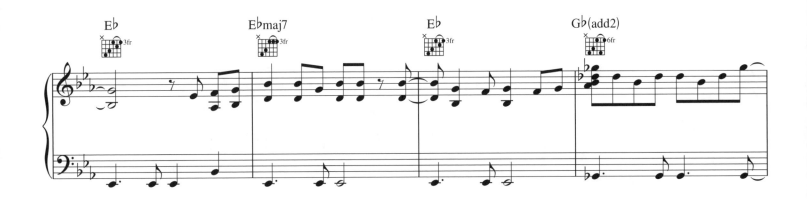

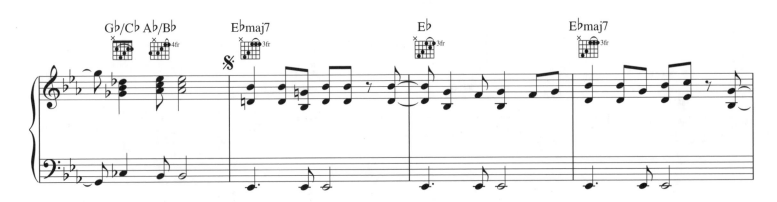

QUINCY
Theme from the Universal Television Series QUINCY

Words and Music by GLEN LARSON
and STU PHILLIPS

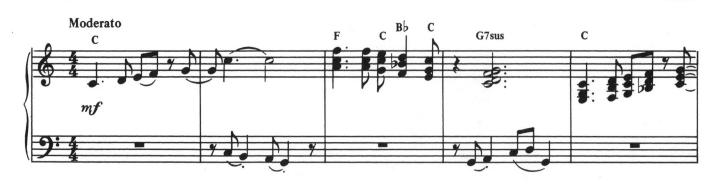

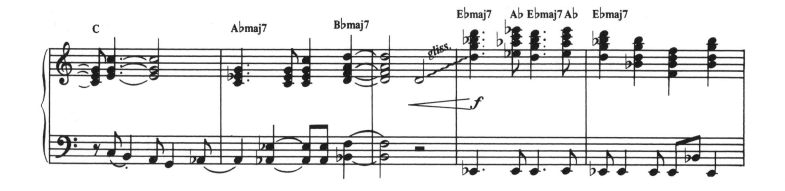

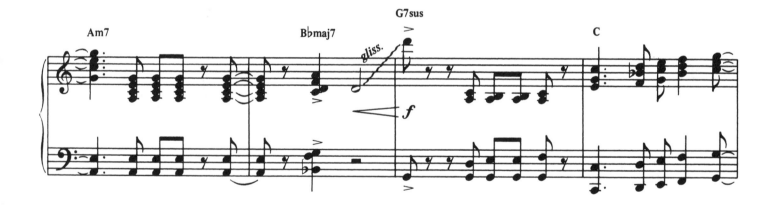

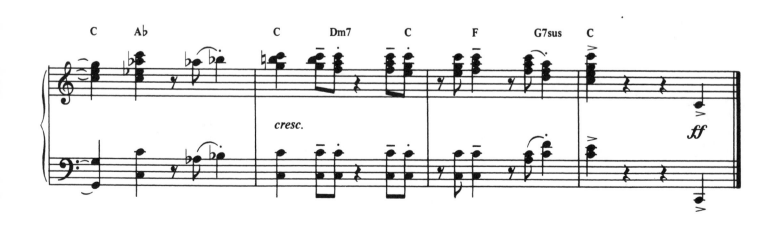

THE ROCKFORD FILES

Theme from the Universal Television Series THE ROCKFORD FILES

By MIKE POST
and PETE CARPENTER

Moderately

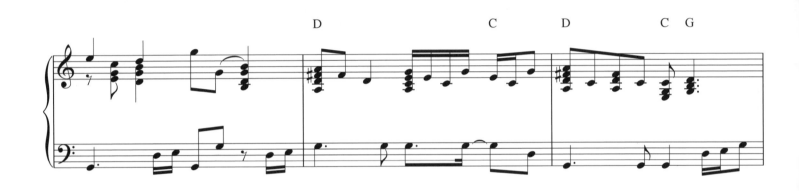

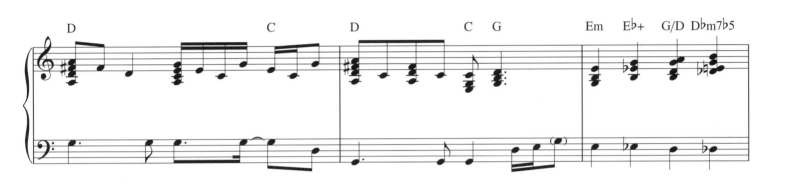

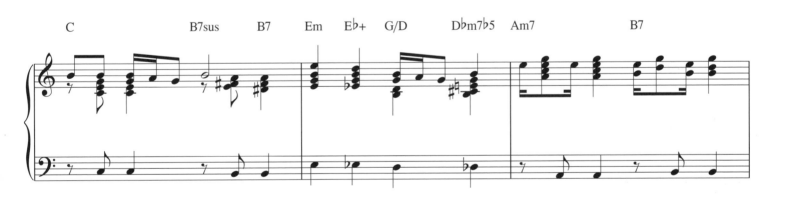

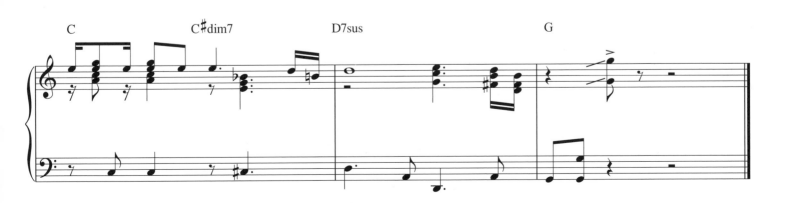

ROCKY & BULLWINKLE
from the Cartoon Television Series

By FRANK COMSTOCK

Rather bright

ST. ELSEWHERE

from the Television Series ST. ELSEWHERE

By DAVE GRUSIN

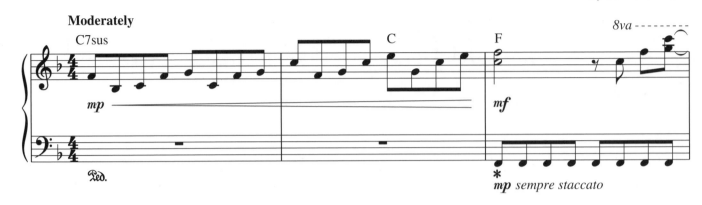

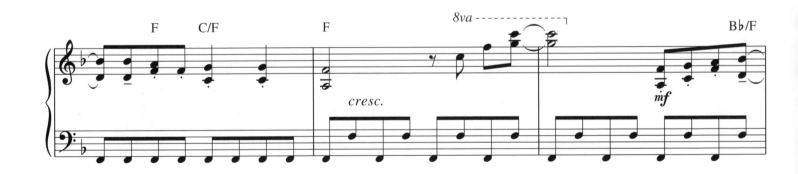

SEARCHIN' MY SOUL

from the Twentieth Century Fox Television Series ALLY McBEAL

Words and Music by VONDA SHEPARD
and PAUL GORDON

I've de- cid- ed to move on. Gon- na leave___ all my wor-

ries___ be - hind.___

SECRET AGENT MAN

from the Television Series

Words and Music by P.F. SLOAN
and STEVE BARRI

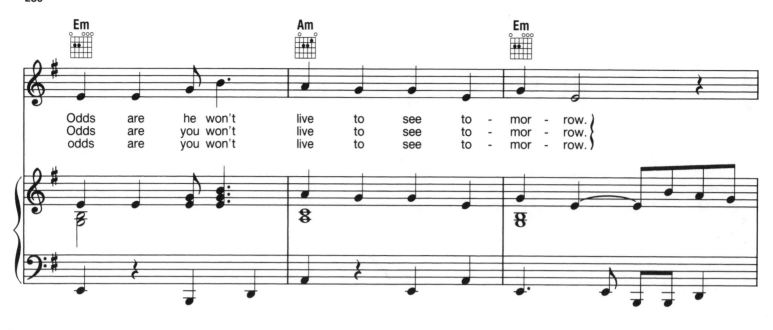

Odds are he won't live to see to - mor - row.
Odds are you won't live to see to - mor - row.
odds are you won't live to see to - mor - row.

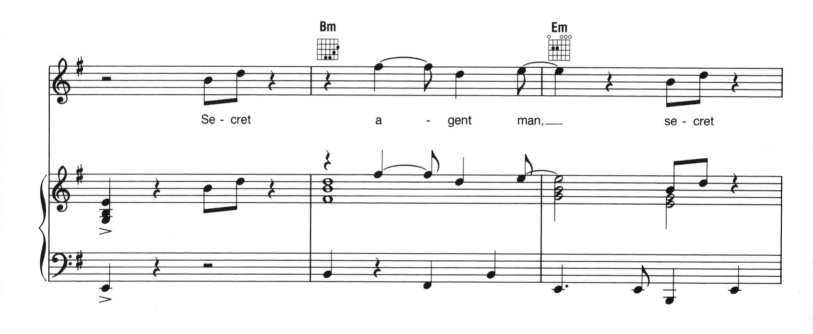

Se - cret a - gent man,___ se - cret

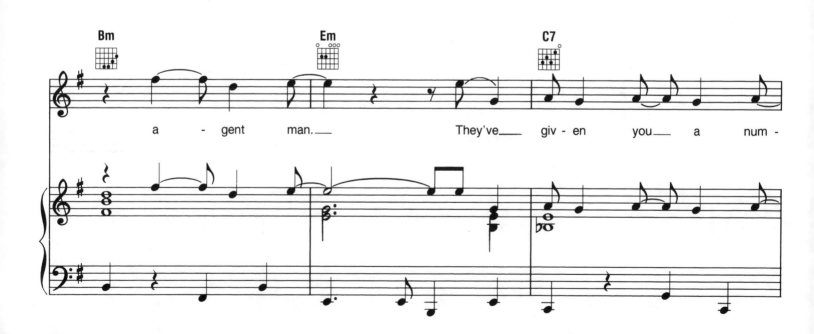

a - gent man.___ They've___ giv - en you___ a num -

SESAME STREET THEME
from the Television Series SESAME STREET

Words by BRUCE HART,
JON STONE and JOE RAPOSO
Music by JOE RAPOSO

THEME FROM "SIX MILLION DOLLAR MAN"

from the Television Series SIX MILLION DOLLAR MAN

By OLIVER NELSON

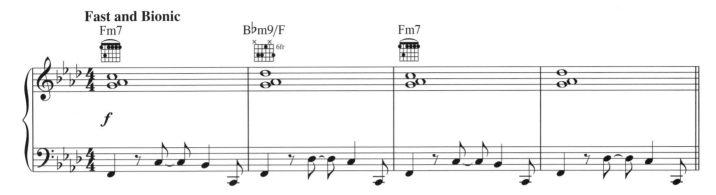

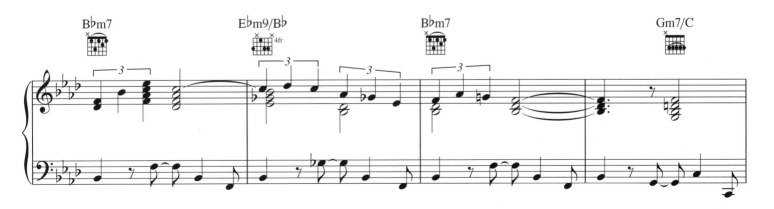

7TH HEAVEN MAIN THEME

Theme from the Spelling Television Series 7TH HEAVEN

Words and Music by STEVE PLUNKETT,
JACK TEMPCHIN and JOHNNY RIVERS

77 SUNSET STRIP
from the Television Series

Words and Music by MACK DAVID
and JERRY LIVINGSTON

Medium Blues tempo

SIMON AND SIMON
from the Television Series

By BARRY DeVORZON
and MICHAEL TOWERS

THEME FROM THE SIMPSONS™

from the Twentieth Century Fox Television Series THE SIMPSONS ™

Music by DANNY ELFMAN

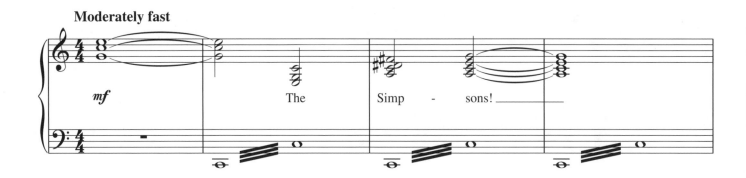

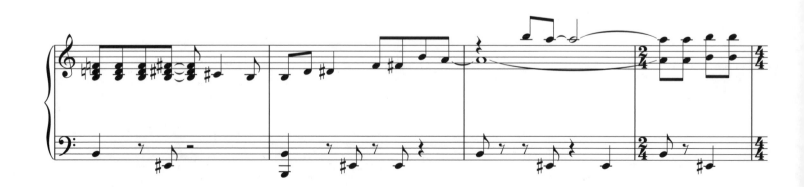

SOLID GOLD
Theme from the Television Series SOLID GOLD

Words by DEAN PITCHFORD
Music by MICHAEL K. MILLER

SONG FROM BUCK ROGERS
Theme from the Universal Television Series BUCK ROGERS

Words and Music by
GLEN LARSON

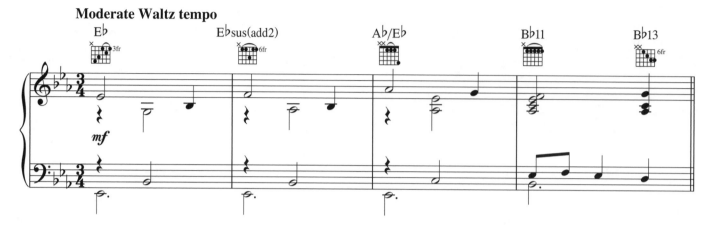

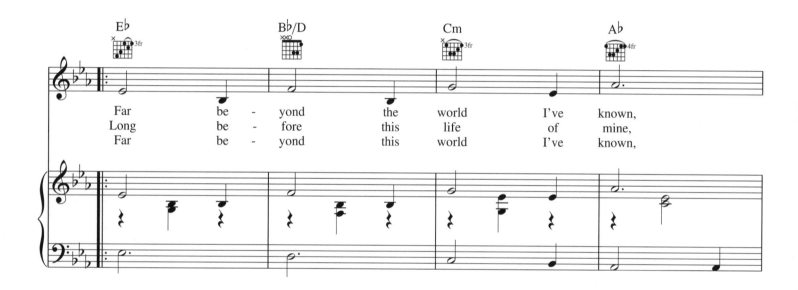

Far be - yond the world I've known,
Long be - fore this world life of mine,
Far be - yond this world I've known,

far be - yond my time,
long be - fore this time,
far be - yond my time,

what am I, who am I, what will I be? Where am I
what was there, who cared to make it be - gin? Is it for-
what kind of world am I go - ing to find? Will it be

go - in' and what will I see? _____
ev - er or will it all end? _____
real or or just all in my mind? _____

Search - ing my mind for some truths to re - veal,
Search - ing my mind past for the things that I've seen,
What am I, who am I, what will I be?

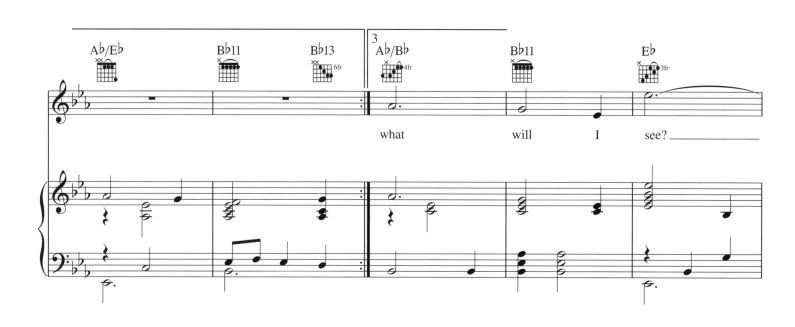

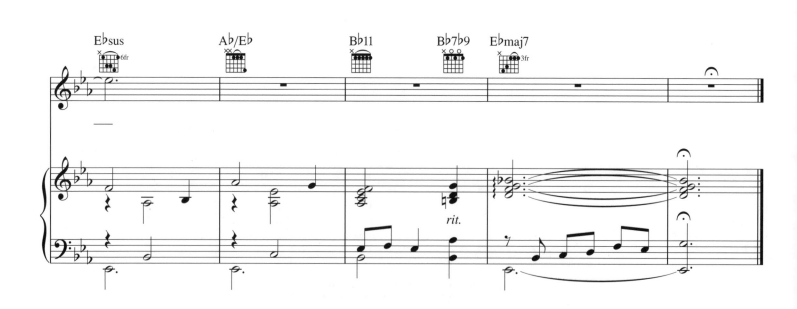

THEME FROM SPIDER MAN

from the Television Series SPIDER MAN

Written by BOB HARRIS
and PAUL FRANCIS WEBSTER

SPONGEBOB SQUAREPANTS THEME SONG

from SPONGEBOB SQUAREPANTS

Words and Music by MARK HARRISON,
BLAISE SMITH, STEVE HILLENBURG
and DEREK DRYMON

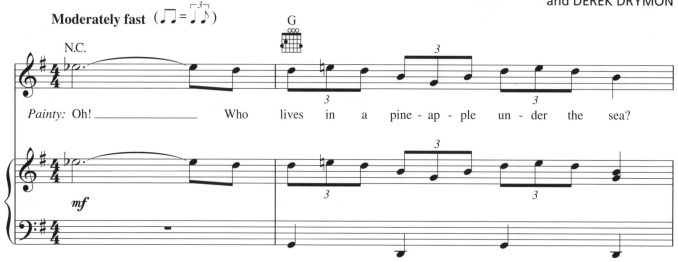

Painty: Oh! _____ Who lives in a pine-ap-ple un-der the sea?

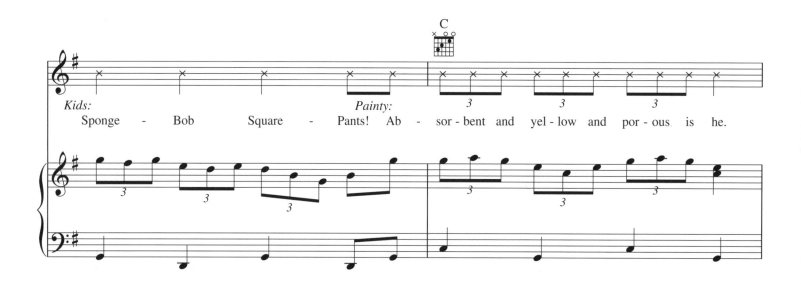

Kids: Sponge-Bob Square-Pants! *Painty:* Ab-sor-bent and yel-low and por-ous is he.

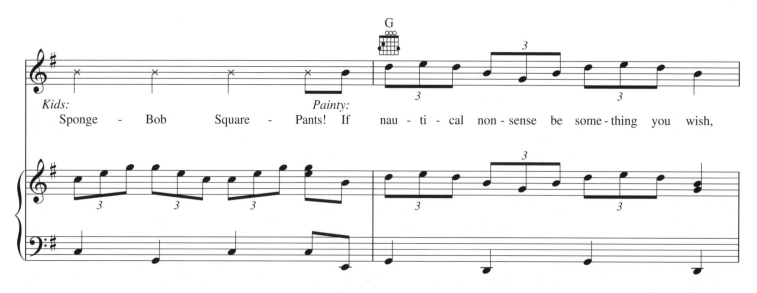

Kids: Sponge-Bob Square-Pants! *Painty:* If nau-ti-cal non-sense be some-thing you wish,

THEME FROM "STAR TREK®"

from the Paramount Television Series STAR TREK ®

Words by GENE RODDENBERRY
Music by ALEXANDER COURAGE

Bright Galactic Beguine

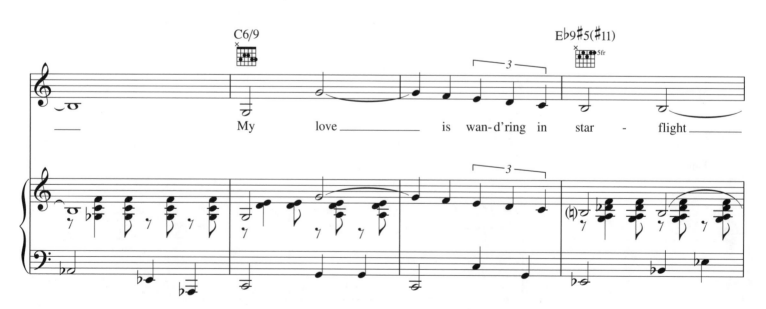

313

TALES FROM THE CRYPT THEME

from the Television Series TALES FROM THE CRYPT

By DANNY ELFMAN

Fast and Spooky

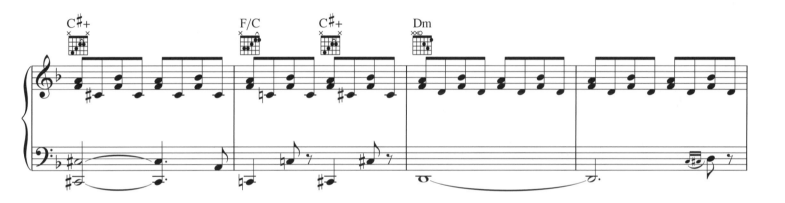

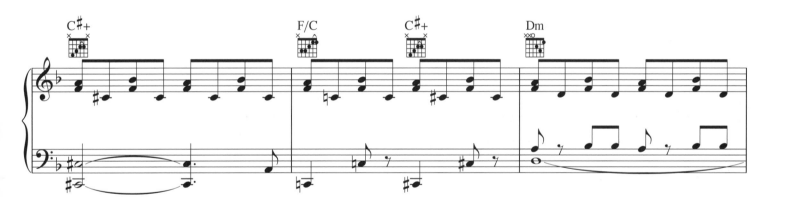

STAR TREK-THE NEXT GENERATION®

Theme from the Paramount Television Series STAR TREK: THE NEXT GENERATION

By ALEXANDER COURAGE,
GENE RODDENBERRY and JERRY GOLDSMITH

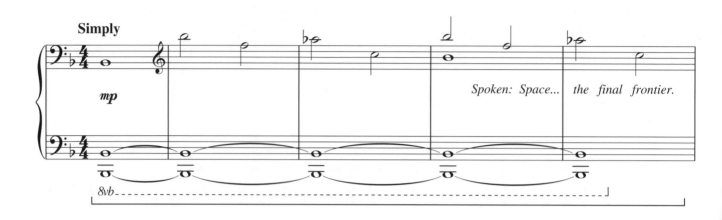

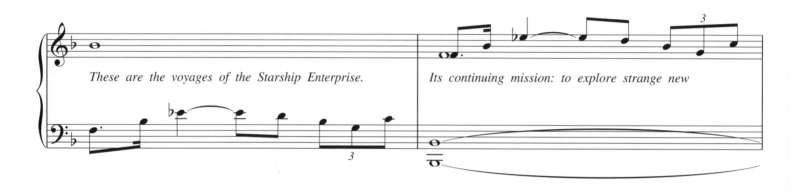

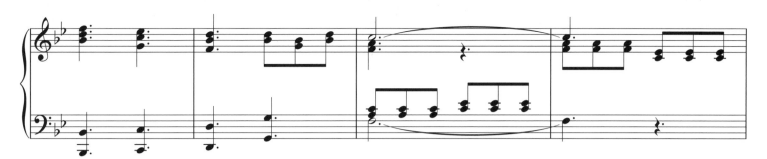

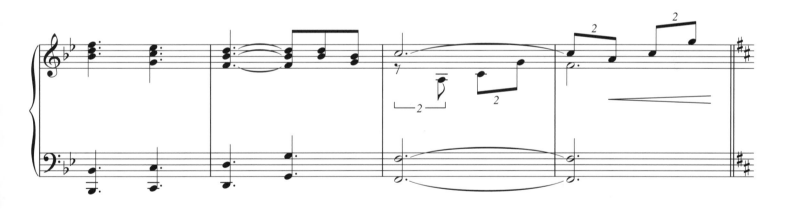

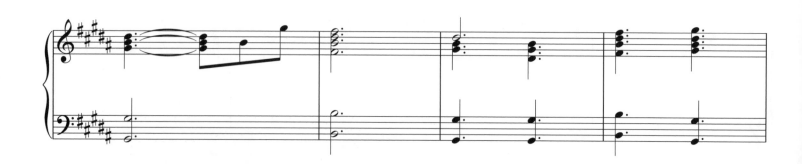

THIS IS IT
Theme from THE BUGS BUNNY SHOW

Words and Music by MACK DAVID
and JERRY LIVINGSTON

Briskly

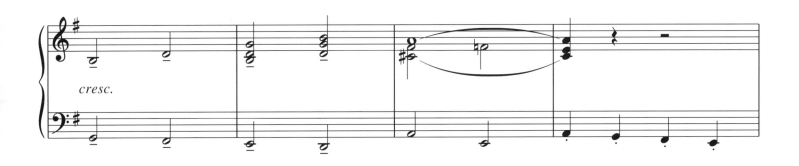

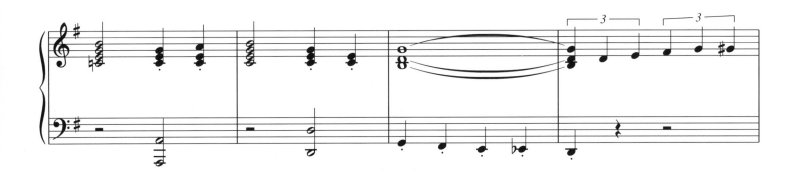

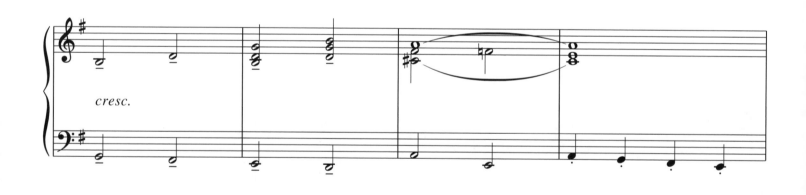

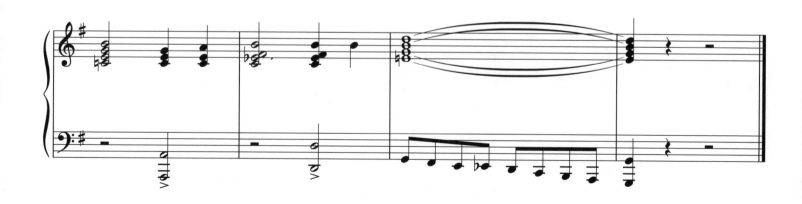

THREE'S COMPANY THEME

from the Television Series

Words by JOE RAPOSO and DON NICHOLL
Music by JOE RAPOSO

Moderate beat

Come and dance on our floor,____

Take a step that is new,____

(Come and dance on our floor.____)   (Take a step that is new,____

THE TOY PARADE
Theme from LEAVE IT TO BEAVER

By D. KAHN,
M. LENARD and M. GREENE

WHERE EVERYBODY KNOWS YOUR NAME

Theme from the Paramount Television Series CHEERS

Words and Music by GARY PORTNOY
and JUDY HART ANGELO

Moderately

Mak-ing your way ___ in the world ___ to-day ___ takes ev-'ry-thing ___ you got. ___
Climb-ing the walls ___ when no ___ one calls; ___ you've lost at love ___ a - gain. ___

Tak-ing a break ___ from all ___ your wor-ries ___ sure would help ___ a lot. ___
And the more you're down ___ and out, ___ the more you need ___ a friend, ___

Would-n't you like ___ to get ___ a - way? ___
when you long to hear a kind ___ hel - lo. ___

WKRP IN CINCINNATI
(Main Theme)
from the Television Series WKRP IN CINCINNATI

Lyrics by HUGH WILSON
Music by TOM WELLS

WELCOME BACK

Words and Music by
JOHN SEBASTIAN

337

WINGS
Theme from the Paramount Television Series WINGS

"Sonata In A" by FRANZ SCHUBERT
as Adapted and Arranged by ANTONY COOKE

WITHOUT US
Theme from the Paramount Television Series FAMILY TIES

Words and Music by JEFF BARRY
and TOM SCOTT

WON'T YOU BE MY NEIGHBOR?
(It's a Beautiful Day in This Neighborhood)
from MISTER ROGERS' NEIGHBORHOOD

Words and Music by
FRED ROGERS

WOODY WOODPECKER

from the Cartoon Television Series

Words and Music by GEORGE TIBBLES
and RAMEY IDRISS

Moderately

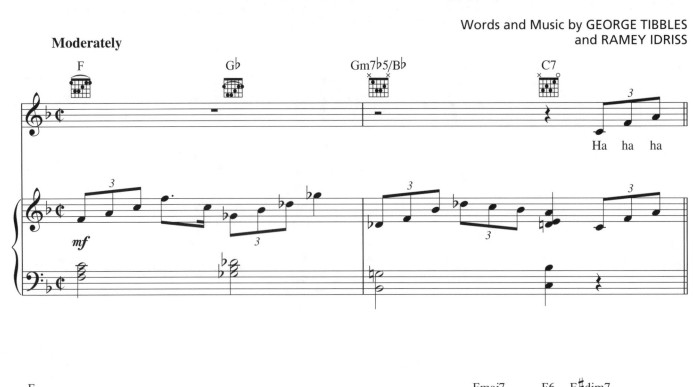

XENA: WARRIOR PRINCESS
from the Television Series

By JOSEPH LoDUCA

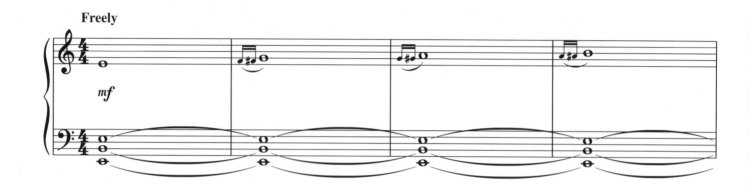

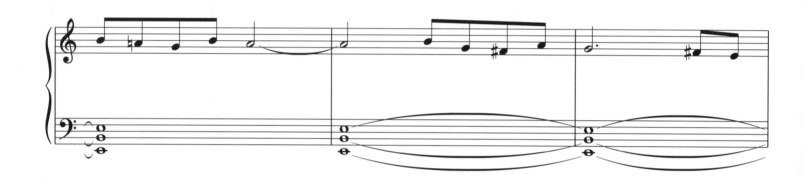

Strong driving beat

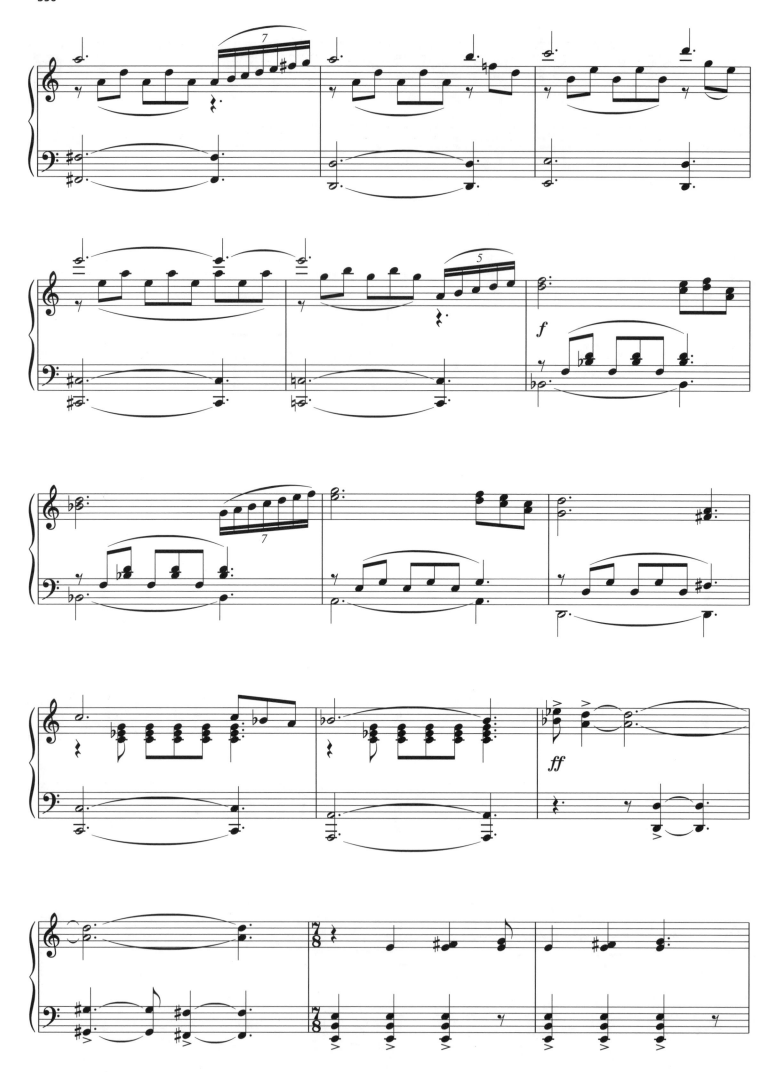

THEME FROM THE X-FILES

from the Twentieth Century Fox Television Series THE X-FILES

By MARK SNOW

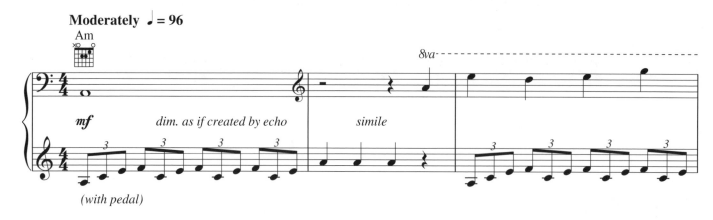

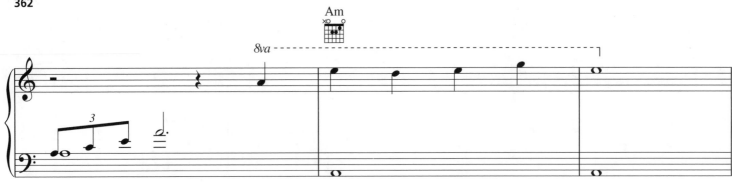
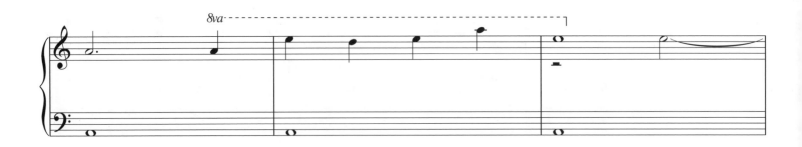
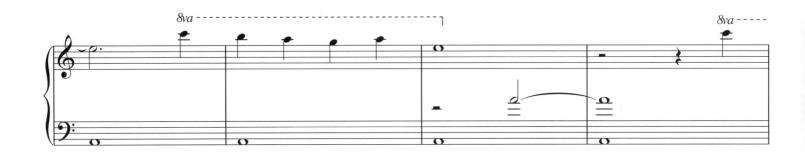
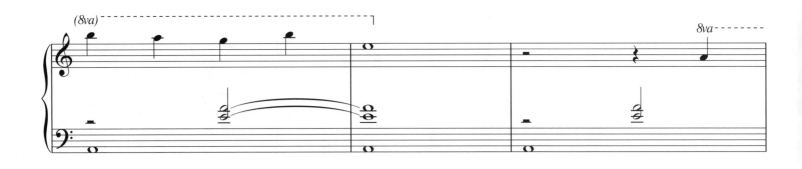
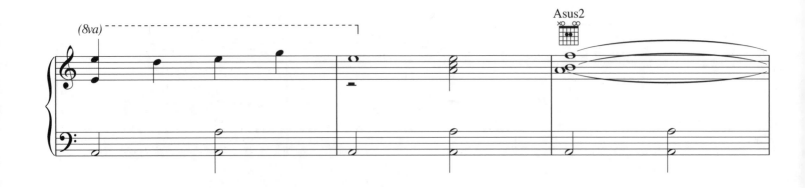

YAKETY SAX

featured in the Television Series THE BENNY HILL SHOW

Words and Music by JAMES RICH
and BOOTS RANDOLPH

With a rocking beat

WOKE UP THIS MORNING

from THE SOPRANOS

Words and Music by JAKE BLACK,
CHESTER BURNETT, SIMON EDWARDS,
PIER MARSH and ROBERT SPRAGG

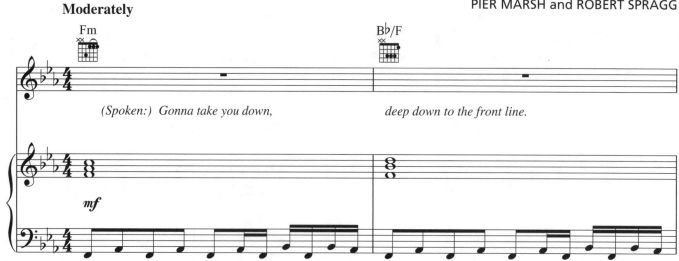

(Spoken:) Gonna take you down,   deep down to the front line.

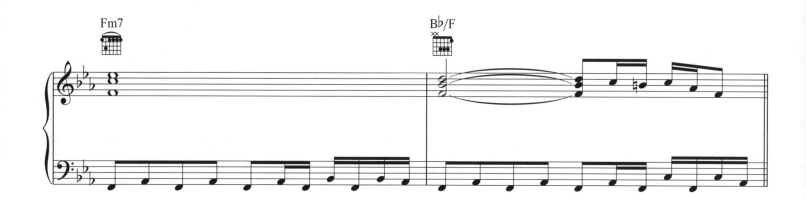

*You woke up this morn - ing, __ got your - self a gun. __
woke up this morn - ing, __ all that love had gone. __
woke up this morn - ing, __ the world turned up - side down, __ Lord __ a - bove.

*Lead vocal sung two octaves below written pitch.

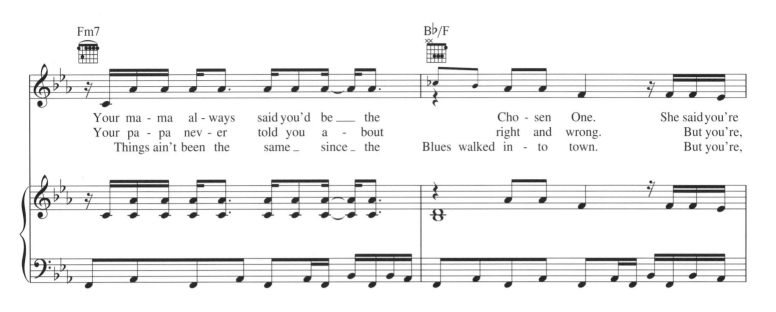

Your ma - ma al - ways said you'd be ___ the Cho - sen One. She said you're
Your pa - pa nev - er told you a - bout right and wrong. But you're,
Things ain't been the same ___ since ___ the Blues walked in - to town. But you're,

one in a mil - lion; you've got to burn to shine. But you were
but you're look - ing ___ good, ___ ba - by. I be - lieve that you're a - feel - ing fine. ___ Shame ___ a - bout it.
but you're one in a mil - lion 'cause you've got that shot - gun ___ shined. Shame ___ a - bout it.

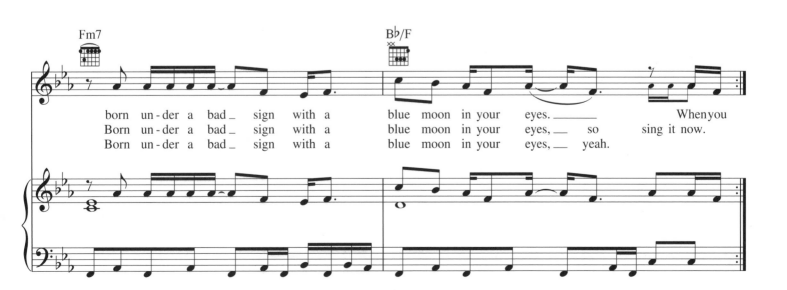

born un - der a bad ___ sign with a blue moon in your eyes. _____ When you
Born un - der a bad ___ sign with a blue moon in your eyes, ___ so sing it now.
Born un - der a bad ___ sign with a blue moon in your eyes, ___ yeah.

You got your-self a gun. ___ You got your-self a gun. ___

Play 3 times

Rap Lyrics

When you woke up this morning, everything was gone.
By half past ten your head was going ding-dong,
Ringing like a bell from your head down to your toes,
Like a voice trying to tell you there's something you should know.

Last night you was flying, but today you're so low.
Ain't it times like these makes you wonder if you'll ever know
The meaning of things as they appear to the others:
Wives, husbands, mothers, fathers, sisters and brothers?

Don't you wish you didn't function, don't you wish you never think
Beyond the next paycheck and the next little drink?
Well you do, so make up your mind to go on, 'cause when you
Woke up this morning, everything you had was gone.